THE MEMO

20 YEARS INSIDE THE DEEP STATE FIGHTING FOR AMERICA FIRST

THE MEMO

20 YEARS INSIDE THE DEEP STATE FIGHTING FOR AMERICA FIRST

RICH HIGGINS

Published by

 CALAMO

The Calamo Press
Washington D.C.

calamopress.com
Currente-Calamo LLC
2425 17th St NW, Washington D.C. 20009
© Copyright by Rich Higgins
All rights reserved

ISBN: 978-0-9997059-2-6

TABLE OF CONTENTS

INTRODUCTION

When I was a surrogate for the Trump campaign in 2016 I frequently used the term Deep State as an all-encompassing term for the forces who opposed the candidacy of Donald J. Trump. And like clockwork, after each speech, I was approached by audience members who would tell me to abandon the term as I came across as a "conspiracy theorist."

I would ask, "do you disagree with my assessment?"

"No, but if you want to be taken seriously you should use a more neutral term."

Well, that was then and this is now. Even the New York Times acknowledges there is a Deep State but we should be thankful for it because it "exists to battle people like Trump."

I guess I was ahead of the curve but I have always called things the way I see them. It didn't matter if I was in a meeting with Secretary Rumsfeld or with President Trump, you can't shy away from telling the truth. Political correctness is a weapon against reason and critical thinking. Our leaders don't usually make poor decisions because they have a nefarious agenda; they do so because those responsible for advising them are afraid to tell the truth. They are afraid to deviate from the party line. And for this, our country has paid a tremendous price.

This book is the story of my twenty year career battling what people now refer to as the Deep State. I want my readers to understand what we are up against from someone who has been in the trenches. I want the tens of thousands of patriots inside the system to learn from my successes and failures and to most importantly understand that you will be rewarded for taking a stand. Many patriots have lost much more than a secure government job in defense of our nation.

The COVID-19 pandemic is an escalation by the Deep State in their efforts to prevent the American people from reclaiming their country. They will do anything to stop us.

Spygate failed.

Russiagate failed.

Ukrainegate failed.

Impeachment failed.

Now the Deep State is going for blood. We can win but we have to view the war through this prism. You cannot view these events in isolation.

The story is a warning, an explanation, a call to arms. I hope you will join me in this fight.

1

BUSTED

Just before I was perp-walked out of the Old Executive Office Building and onto the street in front of the White House, my executioners let me collect the personal stuff from my office. In fact, they were even generous enough to give me a bag I could use for my belongings. It was a sort of shopping bag made from something that I suppose you would call polyester. It was green. The shade of green usually seen in off-brand plastic soda bottles or pennants flying in front of used car lots.

It was ugly and synthetic; you'd think the White House and the National Security Council could have done better than that. But, then, it might have been intentional. A small way of adding to my sense of humiliation. Like dressing me up in a clown suit or something. But probably not—most likely the bag was just handy. Someone in the government had ordered those bags by the gross, not paying attention to the color. Now they had to be used for something.

Anyway, I didn't feel humiliated or disgraced or anything like that. I was angry, of course. But in a very real way, I felt vindicated. Also relieved. Like a soldier no longer at the front. I'd been fired from the National Security Council for the offense of…warning the President…and telling the truth.

I had written a memo about the power and the influence of the Deep State and its intent to remove the President. Little did I know as I walked out of the White House complex, green bag in hand, that the political war for the Trump presidency was only just beginning. I could not have guessed that I would have the opportunity to leverage my twenty years of experience in the National Security field to help President Trump survive the attempts to remove him from office, or that I would eventually return to brief him directly.

The irony was…I was a pure, pedigreed member of the Deep State and had been working in it, and on the front lines of its campaigns, for the past two decades. With a degree in mechanical engineering from Tufts University, I'd gone into the Army where I worked as an explosive ordnance disposal (EOD) specialist. This led to a tour in the White House. From there it had been on to the Beltway and one of those under-the-radar offices in the Department of Defense. I'd been to the rubble pile that had been the Trade Towers twenty-four hours after they had come down. I'd been to Baghdad, devising tactics for dealing with improvised explosive devices (IEDs), the terrorists' deadly weapon of choice, and had briefed people like General James Mattis and Senator John McCain on how those weapons were being used against us in Iraq and Afghanistan.

Many times over those years, seeing the Deep State up close and personal, learning its ways and duplicities, I had felt it might be hopeless. I'd been inside the government and I knew how it worked, and suspected there might just be too many powerful people with too much invested in the status quo for things to fundamentally change. Or that if change did come, it would almost certainly be too late and too little. That there were too many people with power who, if they did not want the United States of America to lose, certainly wanted it to change into something that my father and people like him would no longer recognize.

In short, over the years, working within the system, I had become something of an insurgent myself. I'd fought against policies that came down from the top. First, when I was trying to get us to focus on IEDs and counter-insurgency in Iraq. And then, when I was trying to move our understanding of the role of Islam in what we were calling the "war on terror." But I never tried to sabotage polices I was opposed to or plans that I thought wouldn't work. I tried to reform those policies and change those plans. I did my job as well as I could do it. And I'd never gone after someone and tried to get him railroaded out of the government and sent to prison.

Which is how the Deep State does things.

Although I had been on the National Security Council (NSC) just a few months when I was fired, I had been fully aware of the threat posed by the Deep State long before that. Yet, in my short time with the NSC, I had been eyewitness to a relentless campaign of subversion directed against the President and his agenda. And I was deeply alarmed.

The President had campaigned on an unambiguous agenda of change. The basics included staying out of Syria, defeating ISIS, pulling out of Afghanistan, confronting China, enforcing our borders, rebuilding our economy, and ... well, *Making America Great*

Again. Reversing, in other words, the policies of the last twenty—and more—years that had brought the nation to its dangerous state and which the President had promised to reverse.

The President meant it and some of us were determined to help him make it happen. But ...

The President had failed to understand a fundamental truth. Namely that personnel is policy. And he had failed to purge the holdovers from the Bush and Obama administrations. They remained in place. I worked alongside some of them in the NSC and I knew that if the President did not take the necessary steps, his administration would be a disappointment to his supporters and take the nation further along a road to disaster.

The people in the government who'd opposed his election— and had actively and illegally conspired and worked to make sure it didn't happen—were not going to give up. They would continue to resist even more fiercely after he had been elected and sworn in. For them, it was not "live to fight another day," it was "fight to the death." It was survival. It wasn't opposition, but resistance. And more.

Already, by the time of my dismissal, the Robert Mueller investigation was underway. "Impeachment" was already in the air; not as idle speculation, but as a goal. These people were serious, and they were active. They genuinely thought of themselves as heroic "the Resistance." They were determined to destroy Donald Trump and his presidency no matter what it took.

And they were even doing it within the walls of the White House. I'd seen it and dealt with it every day, and I increasingly felt an obligation—a duty, actually—to make this truth clear to the people, including the President, who needed to know. Keeping my head down just to keep my job was not an option.

So in May of 2017, I put what I knew to be the truth into the form of a memo. I addressed it to those colleagues who had been close to the President during the campaign. I knew that I could not share it with NSC leadership based upon their decisions to date. I hoped that the memo would, ultimately, be read by the President, who would then take the necessary measures.

THE MEMO BEGAN: The Trump administration is suffering under withering information campaigns designed to first undermine,

then de legitimize and ultimately remove the President....

2

THE WHITE HOUSE: MY FIRST TOUR

In a way, my entire professional background was preparation for the alarm I knew had to be sounded against the Deep State.

My two tours of duty in the White House were separated by almost 20 years. Not enough time, it now seems, for the world—and me—to have changed as much as we both did.

In the summer of 1998, I was a 23-year-old Army sergeant trained in explosive ordnance disposal—EOD, in the Army's nomenclature—and my responsibilities were what you might expect. Namely, on-site emergency response to any suspicious packages or possible terrorist incidents along with the checking and screening of packages, parcels, and even people, to make sure that that the President or anyone else in the White House did not get blown up by a bomb someone had smuggled in.

In the world of violent politics, bombs were coming into their own. In South America, the mid-East, Africa. Even in the United States.

The U.S. was technically at peace. After a fashion. But there was plenty going on out beyond 1600 Pennsylvania Avenue. The world is always a dangerous place and there were days back then when it seemed especially so to those of us in my line of work.

On August 7, 1998, terrorists in Africa bombed two American embassies, killing 224 people. The group that was responsible called itself al Qaeda, a name that meant nothing, at that time, to most Americans. The nation was still confident in the existence of what President George H.W. Bush had called a "new world order," in which the United States, the world's only superpower, could be counted on to keep the peace and guarantee stability. Most Americans and the media were primarily concerned with what might, or might not, have been going on between Bill Clinton and a White House intern named Monica Lewinsky. She had begun testifying to a grand jury about her alleged affair with the President the day before the bombings in Kenya and Tanzania.

Those bombings were almost certainly more interesting to me than they were to the average American. I was well trained and had a lot of experience on the range. I thought I knew a lot about bombs but, in the next few years, I would learn a lot more. Especially about what we called Improvised Explosive Devices, the enemy's weapon of choice.

But that was later. In 1998, my work amounted mostly to checking packages and reviewing systems and procedures for screening against explosives. If there was no war between major players going on in the world, that did not mean that terrorists weren't busy and that they weren't detonating bombs with depressing frequency. And not just in the usual places like Ireland, the mid-East and, now, Africa. They were striking the United States as well.

In 1993, there had been a bombing at the World Trade Center in New York. The bomb had weighed more than half a ton and, while it did not quite bring one of the towers down, it came close enough that the building had to be closed down for several months to repair the structural damage. Six people were killed and more than a thousand injured.

The mastermind of the group that carried out the attack, Ramzi Yousef, was eventually arrested and sentenced to life in a supermax prison. Yousef is a jihadi Muslim, as were the other members of his group. This included Sheik Omar Abdel-Rahman who came to be known as "the blind Sheik." He was a Muslim holy man who preached at a mosque in New Jersey. Investigations after his arrest uncovered plots to destroy a lot more than just the Trade Towers. He was planning a war (a *jihad*) against America. Still ... these were the nineties and most people in the United States did not know, or did not really care, what that word meant. They were unaware of the reality that we were already at war. This fact was, however, uppermost in the mind of Ramzi Yousef's uncle, Khalid Shaikh Mohammed, who planned the 9/11 terrorist action that finished the work of that first attack and brought down the Twin Towers.

But ... that came later. Much later. And, as I say, while there were bombings and they did make the news, in the summer of 1998, Americans were living the dot-com boom and following the Clinton scandals. When President Clinton, after the hotel bombings in Africa, ordered retaliatory strikes with cruise missiles against someone named bin Laden, many suspected that he was doing it to divert attention from his own problems, which were domestic in both senses of that word. The cruise missile strikes did not kill bin Laden or even inconvenience him much and probably served to convince him that he was dealing with a weak and ineffectual enemy—a paper tiger.

I wasn't among the cynics who believed the worst about Clinton—that the counter-strikes were done for reasons that had to do with domestic politics and not national security. I was young, but I was also a military man with all that implies about respect for the chain of command and the civilian leadership. To my young mind, the White House had to pay attention to the attacks and take the necessary counter measures.

For my part, it was strictly a matter of "stay alert" and do your job. Our team checked packages, and I specifically recall examining gifts sent to Hillary Clinton from her friends in the Middle East and responding to the occasional package tossed onto the White House grounds. While my memories of those days have grown hazy with time, I'm sure that there were always important people arriving for high level meetings and trailing a retinue of assistants behind them and that I was, almost literally, rubbing shoulders with them. These would be the important players from the Pentagon, the State Department, and the CIA and I would recognize their faces. They were the people responsible for our nation's security and I predictably treated them with respect, but not awe.

I was basically a street kid who had recently graduated from college and joined the Army. Now, here I was, in the White House, in the company of people who were responsible for the safety and security of the United States of America. I was from Boston, and grew up with the statue of a Minuteman in the neighborhood park. My family's house was located on the route of Paul Revere's ride. Yeah. I was patriotic, but in a subtle, earnest way.

My trust in the country's leadership was uncomplicated and pretty simple. They were smart and experienced, I thought, and they would at least try to do the right thing. Still, they put their pants on one leg at a time. Just like me. Harvard, where a lot of them had gone to school, wasn't too far from where I'd grown up. I knew, from stories I heard people tell when I was a kid, how badly people from Harvard had bungled things in Vietnam.

Still, the people I saw in the White House corridors had important and powerful jobs in and out of government. I suppose they might have been part of what we now call the "Deep State." A phrase that, incidentally, I never heard during my first White House tour.

THE MEMO CONTINUED the White House response to the internal threat within the Trump presidency is dangerously inadequate to the threat. If action is not taken to re-scope and respond to these hostile campaigns very soon, the administration risks implosion and subsequent early departure from the White House.

3

FIRE IN THE HOLE

I got out of the Army in 2000, shortly after the end of my tour at the White House and a transfer to California. I'd thought a little about staying in the service and maybe even making it a career. But the peacetime military is always very slow moving and bureaucratic and you spend a lot of time just ... well, spending time. And that wasn't what I wanted.

I was looking for an adventure.

So I sent out resumés and job applications to places where my skill set would be a good fit. When I was stationed in California, I had done a lot of traveling, working with the Secret Service and doing training events with local cops, helping out the bomb squads. I knew some of the players and I had solid engineering and explosive credentials. I was flown back to Washington for an interview with the company I wound up working for, System Planning Corporation. SPC for short.

Its headquarters was in Arlington, in Rosslyn atop the Gannett Tower, not far from the Pentagon. SPC's offices offer sweeping 32nd floor views of the entirety of Washington DC.

I was recently married so my bride and I packed up, drove east, spent a couple of weeks with my family in Boston, then moved into an apartment out in the Virginia sprawl and I started my new career and my new life. It was the Spring of 2000.

In my new job, I was the company's liaison with the Department of Justice and a program called the National Institute of Justice, which manages the DOJ's research and development portfolio.

For the most part, I was going out to help SWAT teams and bomb squads, bringing them up to speed on what was coming along on the tech side with terrorists and explosives. A lot of state and local police departments didn't have the budgets to support R&D programs for handling bombs, so I worked with the FBI's Hazardous Devices School and Bomb Data Center and bomb squads in the police departments in New York, Boston, and Chicago, and kept everyone up to date. There was a lot of networking and sharing of information.

The job was, essentially, to stay on top of what was going on with the terrorist threat world-wide. We conducted forensic studies of the various bombing incidents around the world and developed the necessary countermeasures. We developed something called "disruptors." These are tools a bomb squad uses once it has actually found a bomb. These were not discussed publicly because they included techniques that could be turned back against the bomb squads. Just say that they were sophisticated and effective.

We ran Critical Incident Response Technical Seminars (CIRTS) where we would bring in the tech guys from various bomb squads and have people from the Defense Intelligence Agency (DIA), the

Central Intelligence Agency (CIA), and the Federal Bureau of Investigation (FBI) brief them on the things we were seeing around the world so they would be familiar with tactics, techniques, and technology when something did happen.

We had the tactics and the technology for dealing with terrorist bombings. We were, I think, as prepared as we could feasibly have been. But on the intelligence and policy sides, especially regarding information sharing ... not so much. We were not ready and were shocked and surprised by what happened on what I remember as a beautiful Tuesday morning.

It had been one of those summers that remind you that Washington was, literally, built on a swamp. It had been so hot and so humid for so long that you began to think it would never end and, then, on that morning, the weather finally broke. It was cool. Maybe seventy, seventy-five degrees, with no humidity and clear blue skies.

My wife drove me about a mile from where we lived and dropped me off at the office in Arlington, just up the road from the Pentagon. I was sitting at my desk, working, when my boss, a woman named Mitzi Williams, came in and said "Did you see what's on the television?"

Those words were being apprehensively spoken, all over America.

She was talking, of course, about the plane that had flown into the tower in New York City. So far, it was just one.

Eerily, a few weeks earlier a colleague at SPC had stopped by my office to discuss nuclear threats from terrorist groups. I told him that terrorists were practical, but that if they wanted a mass casualty attack, they would "crash a plane into a skyscraper."

Yes. No question in my mind, it was an attack. Like everyone who worked in terrorism, I was sure of it.

I wasn't watching the television when the second plane hit. But when I heard about it, I said to someone, "Man, this is going to be thousands of dead."

"No," he said. "Not that many."

"Those buildings might be coming down," I said, going on my engineering background.

He just didn't believe it. Didn't understand the scale of the thing. The weight of a 767 and the force when it is traveling at that speed. And all that fuel that it is carrying.

Still, I wish I hadn't been right and that my skeptical colleague had called it.

I spent the rest of the day with Mitzi and a retired Special Forces colonel who worked in our office. The conversation went around and around, going nowhere in particular. We knew a lot about the world and considered ourselves pretty wise about its ways. No rose-tinted glasses. No fairy tales.

Like everyone in the country, we were in shock. Just stunned. Feeling helpless.

When I got home that night, my wife told me that she had come home from the community college she was attending and found our next-door neighbor sitting on her front step, sobbing. When my wife asked if there was something she could do, the woman said, "I just walked home. I don't know where my car is."

My wife had dropped me off at work that morning and attended a language class at a local community college. A student came into the class and told them to turn on their television. The first plane had struck.

The class watched as the second plane hit the towers. At that moment, a student from the class stood up; judging by his appearance he was Middle-Eastern. He walked to the front of the class and in enormous letters wrote "OSAMA" on the chalkboard. Nobody, except my wife, knew why that was significant. She stayed quiet. Class cancelled.

Shocked students stood bewildered in the school's hallway watching events on small televisions. My wife heard a distant rumbling quickly become the screaming roar of a jet airliner as it passed over the school......too low and too fast for a Reagan Airport landing. Much too low. A few seconds later, the third plane would reach its target.

It turned out that our traumatized and sobbing neighbor had been driving by the Pentagon on Route 110 when American Airlines Flight 77 went right over her and crashed into the building. She just pulled over, got out of her car and walked home.

It is still hard to describe what that day was like. The country was in a state of collective trauma. What my neighbor had done seemed ... well, it didn't seem strange or unbelievable or any of those things. A lot people would have probably done the same thing after seeing an airliner come over so low that you thought it might hit you and then watch it crash into a building.

I called my parents, since they knew I was in and out of the Pentagon from time to time. I wanted them to know I was all right. I remember asking my father, "What do you think we ought to do, Dad?"

"Nuke them," he said.

I imagine a lot of people were thinking the same thing.

THE MEMO CONTINUED Candidate Trump's rhetoric in the campaign not only cut through the Marxist narrative, he did so in ways that were viscerally comprehensible to a voting bloc that then made candidate Trump the president; making that bloc self-aware in the process.

4

A FIGHTING POSITION
AGAINST BOMBS
AND BOMBERS

The morning after the attacks, I went to New York and the site of what had been the World Trade Center and was now a hot, smoking pile of rubble.

My bosses at the Justice Department thought we might have something to contribute to what everyone was hoping was a rescue effort. Maybe there were some survivors, trapped in air pockets somewhere in the debris where crews were digging and looking. We had some technology for underground personnel detection, also some ultra-wide band radar systems, some robot technology ... equipment that might help in finding anyone who was still alive inside. I was on the tech side of things and knew the gear so I got the job and rode the Amtrak to New York City the morning after the towers came down. My partner and I were, literally, the only passengers on the train. Those were strange times—spooky, even—and being on that train with just one other person might have been one of the strangest things I've ever experienced. Like arriving in a familiar city and finding it deserted. Empty streets. Empty buildings. No sign, anywhere, of life.

When we got to Manhattan and the scene of the bombing we knew pretty quickly that it was a lost cause. Just hopeless. NY Fire Commissioner Von Essen said to us, "Look, we've got a 2,500 degree fire down there. Massive amounts of smoke. We're dealing with a superheated toxic environment and we're just not seeing anybody because it was a progressive collapse." Anybody who *did* survive, didn't survive long.

Most of the people in those buildings, when they collapsed, were killed instantly. They didn't suffer. I think it's important for people to know that.

Just looking at the rubble pile was a stunning experience. Unbelievable, really, and not in the way most people use that word. It was truly apocalyptic and massive. A 100-foot high pile of rubble where the World Trade Center had stood. There were papers sort of floating in the wind, memos and documents from people's offices. Pulverized concrete covered everything. The leaves had been blown off all the trees in the area and there were blinds from what had been office windows hanging on the branches of those trees where the leaves had been.

There were firetrucks parked around the rubble pile and there were things on the trucks that the firefighters had left behind before they started their climb. Their G-Shock wrist watches. The boots they'd taken off so they could change into lighter footwear. The overboots they had decided not to wear so the climb would be easier. Boots they would never wear again.

It was a haunting image, all those empty boots, and it stayed with me a long time.

I still smoked cigarettes back then and I would sit there with the firefighters when they came off the pile. We'd sit, just smoking. Not saying anything. Those guys were traumatized. In complete shock. All of them had lost friends. A lot of them had lost family members. The FDNY lost the equivalent of two infantry companies in the military. Just wiped out. Everyone KIA. The sort of casualties that are just unheard of.

There really wasn't anything my partner and I could contribute. Not on the tech side, anyway. But we were there and we wanted to help so we made ourselves available and tried to make ourselves useful. We ran errands.

For example, the FBI passed us color photographs of the black boxes that had been on the airplanes and we drove around Manhattan in a Secret Service vehicle, with the flashers on, going to Kinko's and other places to get copies made. The copies were for people working the rubble pile so they would know what the boxes looked like and be able to identify them if they ran across them.

They never did, of course. Those black boxes were obliterated upon impact and any pieces that did survive impact were incinerated in the fire. And, when you think about it, even if we'd found them, what would we have learned that we didn't already know?

Still, we were doing *something*.

We stayed for about a week, doing what we could and what we were asked to do. We were billeted a couple of miles up the West Side Highway in a building located across from the Javits Center, where we slept on army cots and could use the showers. When we would drive back and forth between there and the rubble pile, we would pass the crowds that would be cheering us on. In some people's minds, it was still a rescue effort and we might be finding survivors. And that really stuck with me for a long time, the image of those people who had hope, when I'd been down there and knew that it was hopeless.

As you'd get close to the pile, you would smell it, and then you would feel the heat. The smell was familiar to me from my work with explosives. A kind of acidic, chemical aroma that lingers in the area after a detonation. Gritty and toxic. A smell that is hard to wash off and that you don't forget.

There is another memory that has stayed with me. That is ... the way people and organizations responded. Steel workers, heavy equipment operators, local construction unions ... just heroic. If the call went out for blowtorches, hundreds of them would show up as donations. Businesses like Home Depot were just incredibly generous. Right there, stepping up with whatever you needed or what just might come in handy.

Even though the shock of the event lingered for a long time, people rallied. This was New York, after all, and the people there are just tough. They see a lot of stuff and they deal with it. They deal with the craziness; they deal with the crowds; they deal with the traffic; they deal with all the political garbage that goes on there, and for them to be shocked takes a lot. Still, they had been shocked. No question. But they were already recovering when, after a week or so, I went back to Washington and what we were now calling the "War on Terror."

The phrase is wrong. It might seem a kind of academic distinction but "terror" is a tactic. You don't wage war against tactics. You fight an *enemy*. One of the first principles of war fighting is that you must "know your enemy." Sun Tzu's insight, from *The Art of War*, is

2500 years old and it has held up. If we were at war, after 9/11, not only did our leadership not know the enemy, it couldn't even name him. It didn't *want* to name him.

This wasn't true, however, of everyone who was on what you might call the "front lines" of that war. Some of them – indeed, some of "us" – knew we were at war, and with whom, before the planes ever hit the towers. Everyone in the counterterrorism community knew who the enemy was and that he was already at war with us and always preparing new attacks.

We had the enemy's own words, his own declarations of war, to go by.

Less than three months before the 9/11 attacks, I attended a conference of the International Association of Bomb Technicians and Investigators in Albuquerque. There were maybe 400 of us there. The featured speaker was the ABC News reporter John Miller, who was one of the two Western journalists who had interviewed Osama bin Laden.

The crux of Miller's speech was that bin Laden was planning to attack us.

Here.

At home in America.

The official thinking in those days was that well, yes, he might be planning an attack, but it would most likely be overseas and that it would be against "soft targets." But there were a lot of reasons to think the way Miller did. That is ... that bin Laden was planning an attack on U.S. soil. There was, for instance, the failed attack on the Los Angeles airport in late December 1999, by an al Qaeda operative named Ahmed Ressam. According to Miller, that attack and other evidence—including communications intercepts—pointed to "a significant attack on the U.S....and soon."

I remember sitting there and watching Miller's presentation about bin Laden's most recent video release. It showed bin Laden vowing attacks and cutting to images of the Pentagon, New York, and the Capitol. And I was thinking, "No way. There's just no way they're going to attack *all* of our most sacred buildings."

Along with everyone else in the counterterrorism community, I had no doubt that attacks were coming, like Miller said. And soon.

Still, there were people who should have been listening to those warnings but who just didn't want to hear. It was like Pearl Harbor and Tet and other times when the U.S. has been the victim of a disastrous surprise attack. People high in the chain-of-command simply didn't want to hear warnings from the people somewhere deep down in the system that were doing the heavy lifting. People like FBI agent Colleen Rowley who sent memos to the Director of the FBI telling him about Middle-Eastern males showing up with lots of cash at flight schools in Minnesota and Oklahoma, asking to learn how to fly an airplane but not how to land one.

Sounds like an important clue to me. But what did I know? I was just a bomb tech. A grunt in the counterterrorism world.

So … we had been blindsided and we had to respond. And while Washington confused the issue and resorted to euphemism with that declaration of a "War on Terror," it moved quickly and massively to organize the assets we needed to fight it. And to equip the people doing the fighting with everything they needed. And more. The CIA, the FBI, and all of the services were brought into the effort. The creation of the Department of Homeland Security occurred within days of the attacks and before long it was a cabinet-level office with responsibility for a number of agencies to include, among others, the Coast Guard, the Customs Service and Border Patrol, the Federal

Emergency Management Agency, the Transportation Security Administration, and the Secret Service.

Billions in new money was appropriated, thousands of new bureaucrats were hired. It was a frantic time in Washington. I imagine it was probably something like that in the days after Pearl Harbor when the entire country was mobilized. Not that intense and sweeping, of course, but like nothing the country, and Washington, had seen in recent memory.

I knew that I had a skill set that would make me valuable in the effort and I wanted to get in the fight. I had been to the scene of the attack and I wanted to hit back. And I was trained and skilled in the world of munitions. Improvised and otherwise. And it was already plain that this war, against whomever we were fighting, was not going to be fought with tanks and airplanes and nuclear subs. We were now involved in what would come to be called "asymmetric warfare." We would have aircraft carriers and helicopters and all the rest. They — the enemy—would have small arms and explosives. Especially in the form of "improvised explosive devices." IEDs, as we knew them in the trade. Soon, everyone would be familiar with the acronym.

I kept working for the company that had the consulting contract with the Justice Department and it was good duty. I wasn't wasting time. But I wanted to get into something where I would have a more direct role. I had been in Washington long enough to have polished my networking skills so I put them to work. I made calls and I sent out resumes and generally tried to make things happen. I wasn't shy about it. I'm a creature of the streets and I don't test real high on shy. I worked on the principle that if you want something, then you don't hold back. You work for it and you grab it when it comes within reach.

I was thinking CIA. Or FBI. Or something in the Defense Department. Which is where I wound up, through something called the Tech Support Working Group (TSWG, called Tis Wig). Located within the Defense Department's Combating Terrorism Technical Support Office (CTTSO), the TSWG had been brought along by Vice-President George H.W. Bush in 1983 in response to the terrorist bombing of the Marine Corps barracks in Beirut, Lebanon. That particular IED was called a "truck bomb" and it killed more Marines than any single one-day action since Iwo Jima. Moments later, a bomb blew up in the French embassy killing 58 soldiers. In a few weeks, the French and American "peacekeepers" were on their way out, and gone entirely in four months. The bombs had done what they were meant to do. They were crude and massive—the equivalent of 12,000 pounds of TNT in the case of the one used against the Marines. But they were demonstrably effective – tactically and strategically.

The TSWG was created to study such weapons and the tactics employed in their use and to devise offensive and defensive countermeasures. It was a small, under-the-radar outfit. Very few people knew of its existence prior to September 2001 but it was almost instantly, critical…and busy.

THE MEMO CONTINUED While opposition to President Trump manifests itself through political warfare memes centered on cultural Marxist narratives, this hardly means that opposition is limited to Marxists as conventionally understood. Having become the dominant cultural meme, some benefit from it while others are captured by it; including Deep State actors, globalists, bankers, Islamists, and establishment Republicans.

5

DESCENT INTO THE
MADNESS OF IRAQ

I started up officially with CTTSO in December 2002. Three
months later, we invaded Iraq. There were fears, before we went
in, that Saddam Hussein's forces would deploy Weapons of Mass
Destruction (WMDs), especially chemical and biological agents,
against our troops. This meant nerve gas, among other things. We
took the threat seriously enough that troops in the units that would
be going in were issued protective the Mission Oriented Protective
Posture (MOPP) clothing and masks designed for use in toxic envi-
ronments i.e. gas, chemicals, and biological agents.   Saddam had,
supposedly, also been developing nukes, which we planned to find
and destroy.

Well, there were no WMD attacks on our troops during their
quick march up country and into Baghdad where the giant statue of

Saddam was pulled down in a scene that was broadcast around the world. The real Saddam fled and went into hiding.

While no nukes—no WMDs of any kind really—had been found during the invasion, we kept looking. Just as we kept looking for Saddam. But the invasion looked like a win. One that had cost less and been accomplished more easily than anyone had predicted or expected. So quickly and at such a low cost, in fact, that we were not ready for what came next. We had no plan.

But there were people in Washington who saw this as an opportunity. Especially Secretary of Defense Donald Rumsfeld and his deputy Paul Wolfowitz. In their view, this was more than a military victory. It was a liberation. A chance to create a democratic, multi-ethnic nation in the Middle-East. One that would be a friend and an ally, not only of the United States but also of Israel.

Creating a democracy in Iraq, as they saw it, meant completely doing away with the old order. So the Iraqi military was disbanded, along with the ruling Ba'ath party. And when they did that, the people with their vision of a new and democratic nation of Iraq destroyed the entire civil and educational infrastructure of the society, because it was the Ba'ath Party that had held that country together. Its members were the civil service. They were the engineers. They were the people who made the trains run on time, picked up the garbage, and did everything that an orderly, civil society needs done. And the most dangerous result of this was that the Iraqi military and intelligence guys decided, "Well, you know, if they're gonna screw us over, we're gonna screw them back."

As a result, we weren't liberators any longer. Now, we were the enemy—the occupiers—and they were going to wage war on us. Within days of that fateful decision to remove the Ba'athists, the former Iraqi secret police, the former Iraqi special forces, and

Ba'athist paramilitary militias launched a guerilla warfare and bombing campaign.

We were unprepared and we were way short of the kind of resources it would have taken to conduct a peaceful military occupation of the country. Something, by the way, that we knew how to do. We had done it in Japan and Germany. But it took sufficient resources and a plan. In Iraq, we had neither. The Iraq operational strategy had been dependent upon maintaining a semblance of the civil order and infrastructure and most importantly, the Iraqi Army. Deciding to remove the Ba'ath Party obliterated our operational approach. The initiative was lost.

What we got was an insurgency, a resistance, even if you were forbidden to use the words in the Pentagon. No kidding.

But I'll get to that.

When we invaded and then disbanded the Iraqi military, it was all big-think and grand strategy and, as they say, above my pay grade. I was working in the trenches, down at the tech level, and my problems were with the weapons and the tactics we saw on the battlefields of this war.

With *reality*, in other words. There is nothing more tangibly real than something that will vaporize you. Especially if it is in the hands of someone who is angry and eager to do it and knows how. We weren't talking theory. We were in the real world, with real weapons. And for the next few years, that would become my entire world.

There are examples in history, some of them recent, where a new weapon comes along and changes things in ways that are unexpected and decisive. Before World War One, the machine gun was dismissed as a weapon that was, in the words of one general, "of doubtful utility."

So, of course, the machine gun made the bayonet charge futile and suicidal, bringing on the long months and years of trench warfare. Infantry soldiers had been slaughtered by the tens of thousands while generals tried to come up with something that worked. It turned out to be the tank.

Yet, before World War II, only the generals in Germany seemed to have learned that the tank had made maneuver warfare possible again. So German tanks rolled over the armies of nations whose generals hadn't understood the potential of armor and airplanes in combination.

In Iraq, the weapon that changed the battlefield was the improvised explosive device. The IED.

It wasn't anything new. Booby traps and mines have been around for a long time. They are simple and relatively cheap. There are five basic components to an IED. First, there is the explosive, which in Iraq was an easy thing to acquire. There were old ammo dumps all over the country, with no security and thousands of artillery rounds just sitting there in piles.

In addition to the explosive, you need an initiator. Blasting caps were also easy to come by in Iraq.

You need a power source. A battery works fine.

You need a container. A backpack works. Or a suicide vest. Though not all IEDs in Iraq were triggered by a suicide bomber. Not by a long way. There were other methods that didn't require you to blow yourself up and the best of those involved the last component you need for an IED and that is something that digital technology has revolutionized.

You need a switch. Something that activates the bomb. The way it is, for instance, when a foot soldier steps on a land mine or walks into a trip wire. Or when you light a fuse and wait for it to burn down and reach the initiator.

In Iraq, the availability of advanced switches that could be activated remotely changed everything. Now, the enemy could use a garage door opener or key fob or cell phone to trigger a switch and detonate an IED. They could do so cheaply, and without getting caught.

Digital technology had revolutionized the IED and changed the battlespace in Iraq. Also, in Afghanistan. There was no way the insurgents in Iraq could stand up to American troops in any kind of conventional battle. But they could take out a multi-million-dollar armored vehicle with a device made of parts that cost a couple of hundred dollars. The IED kept the enemy in a fight that it otherwise couldn't win and couldn't afford. And it often kept him anonymous and gave him the initiative in that fight.

There were lots of engagements where we lost men and expensive equipment and the only cost to the enemy was that few dollars' worth of material it took to build that IED.

Think about it from the troops' point of view. In a conventional action, you are in a convoy and you get ambushed by, say, a platoon of insurgents. They have rifles and grenades. There is a firefight. You dismount, call in artillery and air support, then you assault the ambush and win the fight. This is good for morale, even if you take some casualties, and you are now that much closer to the ultimate goal, which is victory. Or at least chasing the enemy back into his hole.

But in that same kind of action, if the enemy attacks with an IED, detonated remotely, there is no one to assault and kill. You have a damaged or ruined vehicle. Casualties, to include possible killed in action (KIAs). And the enemy—who has taken no casualties unless the attack was made by suicide bomber—has demonstrated to the local population that you, their supposed liberators, cannot provide the security you have promised.

After you've been attacked, you go back to patrolling, waiting for the next IED to take out the next vehicle, killing and wounding more of your troops.

So, you drive faster and avoid the main roads. You build walls. You spend more and more time and resources finding and clearing these devices and less on directly engaging the enemy. You over-react to what you think are threats. The IED now dictates your tactics. It is a disruptor and it changes everything.

In Iraq, the guys who were in the most danger, taking the greatest risks and taking the most casualties, weren't the elite operators or the ordinary infantry troops. They were the guys whose Military Occupational Specialty (MOS) was 88 Mike. The truck drivers. They were some of the bravest guys you saw over there.

The terrorists blew up truck convoys routinely. And sometimes they liked to film the show.

They would have video of the results. Images of wrecked vehicles. Wounded and dead troops. And they would put the video up on the internet to show the world, and especially the people back in the States—whose sons were driving those trucks in Iraq—that the insurgents were not just fighting back but possibly winning.

The IED was simple old explosives, married to modern digital technology, and it was deadly. Seventy-five percent of all casualties in Iraq were caused by IEDs. Fifty percent of all casualties in Afghanistan were caused by IEDs. The only reason a lot of the wounded weren't KIA is that they were medically evacuated (*medevaced*) so quickly and the trauma treatment they got was so good. In previous wars, like Vietnam, many of them would have died from their wounds. Still, the effects of those wounds were horrible. Permanent brain damage. Amputations, often of multiple limbs. Blindness.

The nature and the scale of what IEDs were doing in Iraq was clear pretty soon after the administration claimed "Mission Accomplished" in Iraq. In July there were maybe 50 attacks. In August, there were 300. In September, there were 700. In October, there were a thousand.

My office got an urgent request for assistance in dealing specifically with the IED problem. Were there technological and tactical countermeasures that we could devise and that could be implemented quickly and effectively?

My boss told me to put together a team and get over to Iraq.

A much younger looking Rich Higgins

I arrived in Baghdad at the end of the summer with a couple of former SEALs who I'd recruited. I also brought some additional support. Former CIA guys, a British intelligence specialist, and some folks from the Los Angeles Police Department. There were seven of us. We were billeted at Camp Red Sox out by the Baghdad airport, near one of the tributaries of the Tigris River on the grounds of what had been one of Saddam's sons' palaces. The small palace included a small zoo, where Saddam's son Uday fed his political opponents to the lions. The animals were all gone. Escaped, I suppose. Or killed.

The main building of this river palace complex was maybe six to ten thousand square feet with a big open area inside where the FBI had set up a tactical operations center. Across the street from that, there was this big maintenance area with a garage for trucks and other equipment. And then there were a bunch of little rooms that were made into offices.

We spread out our gear and our bunks in some of those rooms and went to work. Everything was still very ad hoc and jury-rigged at that point in the war. The insurgency was still growing and we had not yet caught Saddam, yet. It was Wild West time. Bombings— multiple bombings—every day. We were struggling just to get our hands around things. Everything was very reactionary. We were a long way from having the initiative.

We ended up becoming the Combined Explosive Exploitation Cell (CEXC)—"sexy" for short. It was the unit that started to bridge the gap between the EOD units that were dealing with the threat— the actual bombs—and the intelligence community that was trying to glean information from the bombs themselves. We wanted to involve the Army, Marines, FBI, Joint Special Operations Command (JSOC), the CIA, the DIA…anyone with some skin in the game.

This was how we were going to deal with the bombing campaign and we were building it up from nothing.

That was the plan, anyway. But in the beginning, it was just seven guys and a pickup truck. When we needed something, we had to ask. We weren't at the top of anyone's hit parade. But we understood our mission. And how important it was. Even if, at first, we were the only ones who did.

Meanwhile, life went on in Iraq. But you wouldn't call it "normal" life. Rockets and mortar attacks were common. Harassing fire mostly. Sporadic and imprecise.

A loud but brief volley of ferocious automatic weapons fire roused us one evening. This was followed by a quick reaction force of two tanks moving toward the special operations compound a half-mile down the road. A few minutes later the tank returned. We waved down the tank driver and he stopped.

"What happened?" we asked.

The tanker yelled over his idling Abrams, "some hajis decided they were going to raid Camp Red Sox tonight. Jumped the wall right into the Special Forces compound." Bad move.

Asta lasagna. Don't get any on ya.

Other than that, things were *relatively* calm.

What we were really focused on was getting after the guys making these bombs. Them, and their networks. There was an acronym from those days…High Value Target (HVT). These were the people who were critical to the insurgency and we went after them with airstrikes, drones, and nighttime raids by the "door kickers" from various combat units. Basically, anything that worked and would take down those people.

There was, of course, the "HVT Bar" at Baghdad Airport. Oddly, Soldiers and Marines were not allowed. The Command had issued specific guidance. "Thou Shalt Not Drink Alcohol" was General Order number #1. The HVT bar was located in an area adjacent to the airport and controlled by one of our intelligence agencies. It was not much more than a plywood shack where you could go to have a beer and unwind and talk about the only thing anyone ever talked about: the war.

The enemy was waging its war with IEDs. That meant that any bomb maker was an HVT. I saw my mission as one of using the bombs, themselves, to lead us to the bomb makers so we could take them out.

We were not a quick reaction force, though we would sometimes travel to the site of a bomb attack immediately after we'd been alerted. But that was rare. There were EOD guys and regular troops on site who would do the things that had to be done right away. They would bring back everything they could collect that would be useful to us. Then we would do a kind of comprehensive, after-action analysis. So, how did the enemy conduct the attack? Did he use an L-shaped ambush? What type of weapon systems? What type of transmitter? Did he use homemade explosives? What were they? If he used a homemade detonator, what were the components? If he used a commercially available detonator, what was that? What were the lot numbers? Is the structuring of the dual tone multi-frequency receiver unique? Is there a way this guy is making the device that shows up again and again? Is it always on the same part of the spectrum on the transmitter?

We were after every single little detail we could get that would help us build a profile of the bomb maker. Right down to the biometrics. Fingerprints. Hair. Anything that would yield a DNA sample.

These are things that give the person, or persons, who built the bomb away. Little signatures that, maybe, will tell you the guy who made this bomb made one that was used in another attack a few days earlier.

Over time, you began to see patterns. You see that there are more and more attacks were happening in, let's say Ramadi and of 30 attacks 15 of them looked exactly the same. And you could begin to take steps based on the information you'd assembled and the deductions you made from that information. We have an insurgent cell operating in this area here. And they're using these types of tactics with these weapon systems. And that informs your searching, right? So, units that are out patrolling, well, they're looking for individuals that have, for instance, 155-millimeter projectiles. Has anybody found any weapon stores with those? When you interrogate people, ask them about these attacks.

You are trying to generate intel that gets you into their networks. There's a clandestine infrastructure that's behind these attacks and you're trying to get into that. You look at anything and everything. From the operational design of the attack down to the way the weapon is configured.

It's a comprehensive look. The way I described it when I briefed people on what we were doing is that when that terrorist raises his head above the parapet to take a shot at you, he leaves something behind and you need to make as much use as you can from whatever he leaves. That's why it was so important to concentrate on these attacks and take them apart, down to the last detail, because it's one of the few areas where you can get information that will be useful to you further down the road as you're trying to disrupt and destroy these networks. That means finding and detaining—or killing—the right guys. Because you don't want people who know how to build these weapons to be teaching others.

I pushed hard on this, both when I was in-country and, then, back in the States. This was a new kind of high-value targeting, and it was something like what worked in fighting the drug cartels where, if you can go after the head of the cartel, he'll just be replaced by the next guy in line.

But if you go after the specialists who are limited in number, like the money launderers, accountants, and guys who provide functional capability to these organizations … well, their removal severely diminishes that network's ability to recreate itself or expand. That was the big push that I was trying to make – getting us to focus on the bad guy bomb techs. The specialists. The ones who were both the most dangerous and the hardest to replace.

It was no easy thing, either. We were dealing with very capable and creative guys in their ability to adjust to our countermeasures. Like a jamming capability, for instance. They would detect what frequencies we were jamming and then create another device with different capabilities. It was a battle in the electronic spectrum and it was very intense. Countermeasures would result in counter-countermeasures.

Focus on the bomb-makers required the creation of new intelligence approaches and capabilities. One that prioritized forensic and biometric based intelligence. Easy to say. Hard to do.

I worked with my colleagues to initiate what would become known as "The Cerberus Project," named after the mythological three-headed dog that guards the gates of hell. The concept was simple enough. Create a national Terrorist Explosive Device Analysis Center (TEDAC), create multiple Combined Explosives Exploitation Cells (CEXCs), and create tactical units to augment EOD teams with intelligence collection support (Weapons Intel Teams).

The project took the better part of two years to reach initial operating capability. But after a series of small but significant targeting successes, the project took on a life of its own.

I had learned a valuable lesson. The institutions want to protect their missions and their budgets. Today, the FBI hosts the TEDAC in Alabama and the Army's Intelligence and Security Command hosts the weapons intelligence teams. Convince the institution to follow its own doctrine and self-interests, and they will make the mission.

There is no telling how many bad guys we eliminated or good guys we saved; I just assume it was substantial. I still consider this my greatest contribution to the US counterterrorism community and I am grateful to all the patriots who worked alongside me to make it happen.

Starting small allowed us to survive in the bureaucratically charged environment and success bred support. Important lessons for what was to come.

That first trip to Iraq was my longest and easily the most intense. Not in terms of physical danger, although there was always a chance that this was the day that your convoy would be blown up or your headquarters would be mortared.

While I was there, Paul Wolfowitz, the Deputy Secretary of Defense, came over for one of those inspection tours and the hotel where he was staying was hit with rockets. One of his staff was killed. But that was just life and death in Iraq. And, like I said, the guys who were in the most danger were the ones driving the trucks.

Also, even if you were in a relatively "safe" billet, there was the intensity. The pressure and the stress eventually got to people. All war is ugly, and that one could sometimes seem especially so.

The aftermath of an IED attack wasn't something you got used to, even if you'd been exposed to it before. Many times. Bombs do horrible things to the human body. Almost anyone who was ever there has moments seared into their memory which sort of sum up all the horror. One of my own memories is of the very first device I examined while I was there. All these years later, I still remember staring at it when it came in and how it struck me as such a simple little thing. Just a basic command detonated device.

The insurgents had been studying our convoys and they knew that our tactics included driving past the initial IED attack for 500 meters before stopping on the side of the road to assess damage. Well, the insurgents set off an initial small IED.

Then waited.

In the shadows.

At the point where the convoy stopped, 500 meters up the road, there was a second device. A large one. It used eight 155mm projectiles daisy-chained together. The soldiers dismounted their vehicles to assess the damage from the initial attack. A press of a key FOB. Instant carnage. Nobody to shoot back at. Only the dead and wounded to care for.

They had used a simple car key fob and powered their device with a motorcycle battery. It killed three guys instantly and badly wounded another fifteen.

I remember it because it was the first. But there were a lot more after that one.

And, then, there would be the one thing, after all the other things, that would cause someone to just lose it.

We had something like that happen one day when a suicide bomb had killed a bunch of Iraqi kids. The scene was bad enough but what tore it for one of our technical guys was when an EOD guy showed up carrying a zip lock bag with the bomber's hands in it. Just the hands. The sight of that was just too much and the guy lost it. Completely.

He didn't get over it and had to leave country. But we needed those hands to get the latent DNA and fingerprints and then check them against the global database. The paradox of the primal and the advanced. You try to be professional about it ... but still.

The bad memories don't go away then. Not entirely anyway. And on top of them, for me, there was the frustration of always thinking you were behind the curve. Always feeling "not enough." We never had enough time, of course. We felt like we had to get on top of things yesterday, when tomorrow was already bearing down on us. And we never had enough resources. Not enough people. Not enough equipment or the right equipment. We felt short-handed and under equipped, and we were always struggling to catch up. We did the best we could and we did very good and very important work. We did as much as we possibly could with what we had.

But we were just a few guys—seven of us on the team. We were working out of a garage behind the FBI building, driving around in a beat-up old pickup, and trying to get a handle on these bombs that are killing hundreds of Americans. We had no resources. Command wasn't interested in us. It was still focused on the hunt for WMDs and spending, literally, billions on the futile search. They were like those generals on the Western Front in World War One, still dreaming of cavalry charges when the machine gun had changed war and was slaughtering their troops.

We failed to know our enemy. And we failed, for a long time, to appreciate and understand his weapon of choice. And our early failures, while I was there, would later attract bigger problems. These problems included Iran providing sophisticated Explosively Formed

Penetrators (EFPs) under the guidance and direction of Quds Force General Soleimani as well as an increasing role for al Qaeda amongst the Sunni tribes.

I went back to Washington after four months. At first I considered it my mission to change the way we approached and dealt with the weapons. Later, my thinking moved on to how we saw and dealt with the enemy.

Neither approach won any popularity contests for me.

THE MEMO CONTINUED The successful outcome of cultural Marxism is a bureaucratic state beholden to no one, certainly not the American people . With no rule of law considerations outside those that further Deep State power, the Deep State truly becomes, as Hegel advocated, God bestriding the earth.

6

A FIVE-SIDED
PUZZLE PALACE

It was early in 2004 when I left Iraq and went back to Washington. Things in Iraq had been out of control but, then, it was a country at war. The worst sort of war, where atrocities were almost the point. On any given day, an armored convoy might be the target of an IED. But, then, a group of kids might be, too. And the people setting off the bombs didn't seem to see any difference or make any distinctions between the two. Terror was the point and either target worked. Blowing up kids might even be better than blowing up a HUMV.

People routinely described the situation as "insane." And it was hard to argue with that.

Nobody was blowing up kids in America when I got back home. But there were plenty of days when Washington seemed "insane" in its own way.

It took the form of denial. And not just your garden variety of denial, which is to ignore something obvious and unpleasant and simply pretend it doesn't exist. Denial in Washington, when I got back there, took the form of actively insisting that what was happening in Iraq … well, that it wasn't *really* happening. That people who had seen it happening, like me, were simply wrong. And worse. That in some cases it wasn't just that we were mistaken or confused, but that we were acting out of bad motives. That we weren't good "team players." And worse.

And what was it, exactly that was being denied?

The answer to that one is both simple and complex.

At the simple end of the spectrum, people in Washington were denying that what Iraq was going through was an "insurgency."

In the Pentagon, that word was simply not spoken. People in authority had forbidden its use in describing the situation in Iraq. And I mean people at the very highest levels. The absolute top. And this ban applied, if you can believe it, to the most senior commanders in the Pentagon.

Consider this story:

The Secretary of Defense stands up in front of reporters for a press conference about a year and a half after the fall of Baghdad, when the bombing campaign is full-on, and he makes an announcement: We are going to stop calling the people who are indiscriminately blowing up HUMVs and children "insurgents."

"Over the weekend," Donald Rumsfeld explains, "I thought to myself, 'You know, that gives them a greater legitimacy than they seem to merit.'

He added that…"It was an epiphany."

He told the people to consult the dictionary where an insurgency is defined as a "rising up against established authority."

"These people aren't trying to promote something other than disorder," he went on, "and to take over that country and turn it into a caliphate and then spread it around the world. This is a group of people who don't merit the word 'insurgency,' I think."

Standing next to Rumsfeld was the Chairman of the Joint Chiefs of Staff, General Peter Pace. He gets asked a question and is describing the fighting in Iraq. He comes to a place in his answer where he pauses, then says, "I have to use the word 'insurgent' because I can't think of a better word right now."

Rumsfeld cuts in with, "'Enemies of the legitimate Iraqi government'—how's that?"

General Pace shrugs and says, "What the Secretary said."

Everybody laughs.

Funny, maybe, in that room. Not in Baghdad. The guys driving those trucks in the convoys that were getting blown up by IEDs—the 88 Mikes—they weren't laughing.

Some of the people at that press conference may have been thinking that it was just another example of the way the government likes euphemisms and uses fancy language when plain talk ought to do. But this was a lot more serious than that. You could say that it went right to the heart of what was wrong with the war in Iraq and the policies created and executed by the people who had planned it and were running it.

In their minds, it was a war of liberation. The people were oppressed.Saddam was the oppressor. He and his Ba'athist party apparatus that ran the government and the military. They had been defeated, easily, in the "shock and awe campaign," and now it would be just as easy to replace them with some sort of democratic equivalent. Just like that, Iraq would become a democracy. An ally of the United States and a friend of Israel.

Well, they had gotten it wrong. But they were in what people call denial. They weren't just denying it to the reporters and the American people. They were actually denying it to themselves.

I'd been through my own education about this, seen it up close and from the inside. I'd seen what was happening when I was in Baghdad, helping set up the unit, studying forensic evidence and trying to get a handle on the IED problem. Recognizing the reality didn't make me some kind of genius. Most people who were on the ground over there saw it. We knew bullshit when we were standing in it.

The official line from the Pentagon and the rest of the administration, including the White House, was that we were fighting "terrorism" in Iraq. That fallacy, again. Bomb tech training taught me to view any incident or attack through the eyes of the enemy. Hard to do when you refused to acknowledge him and didn't respect him.

So the IED attacks were simply random acts committed by terrorists – specifically al Qaeda – and not an organized resistance. We were not, then, facing an insurgency and we didn't have to create a plan and a structure for dealing with it. It might be necessary to come up with some better armor for our vehicles, so they could survive an IED blast. And we still needed to find those WMDs. But other than that ...

Well, like I say, I knew that was wrong. We needed to understand what we were up against and come up with a plan for dealing with it. At my level, that meant getting all the players looped in. We needed a new level of co-operation and communication among, say, the FBI, CIA, DIA, JSOC, and so on. All of us would develop and share information we gained from studying the IED attacks with the objective of learning who the bomb makers were and what methods they were employing. This would make it possible for us to come up with counter measures and to capture and kill the bomb makers. If we captured them, this would yield more information. If we killed them…well, they would be dead and not building any more IEDs or training the next crew of bomb makers. A win, either way.

But before we could do this, we had to understand what we were up against and the word for that is … "insurgency." And what follows, logically, is that you adopt counter-insurgency measures and tactics. This means you become a lot more like a police and law enforcement operation and less like a military occupation. You begin depending on police tactics. You develop informers. You make arrests and conduct interrogations. You treat the locations where attacks took place as crime scenes and you mine them for evidence. You provide security for the local populations and develop relationships and rapport with people in the communities and you rely on them for information, which they will be a lot more willing to provide once they feel safe.

These are not the things that the American Army had been trained to do. It considered its mission to be war fighting at the heavy end of the scale and it had gotten very good at it. Success in the two wars against Iraq was testimony to that. But that was conventional, big unit warfare with an emphasis on firepower and maneuver. That's what was meant by the phrase "shock and awe."

That doesn't work when you are fighting an insurgency. At least not when using tactics acceptable to Americans.

The Marines have more of a history and tradition for this kind of warfare, going back to when they were developing their small war doctrine and tactics during the early days of the 20th century in what were called the "Banana Wars." But it would be a while before even the Marines began to treat what we were dealing with in Iraq as an insurgency. Because everything came down from the very top, meaning the Pentagon. A couple of months after my return from Baghdad, I got an education in what we were up against. And I don't mean from the enemy we were fighting in Iraq. I'm talking about our own senior leadership.

Not too long after I returned from Iraq, our office was told that the Deputy Secretary of Defense wanted a briefing on what we were working on. We were told there would be other high-ranking Department of Defense (DoD) types at the briefing—so we would be playing in the big leagues.

Which was fine with me. I'd been working the IED problem and the insurgency problem long enough and hard enough to feel confident about my conclusions and recommendations. And I've never been the shy, retiring type. A chance to explain things to this sort of audience was exactly what I was hoping for.

That old naive belief was at work: "If I could just *explain* things to the people in charge, then they would surely understand and do the right thing."

So I went to work, full out, and put together the briefing. Talking points. Visuals. The big day comes and we head over to the Pentagon and the E-Ring where the briefing will be taking place. For those who aren't familiar with the nomenclature: the E-ring is the outermost of the five rings that make up the Pentagon. The offices on the E-Ring are the only ones with windows that had a view of the world outside. Those offices are for the most senior people. They are where the big things gets done and the big decisions get made.

When we get there, the people above me in the chain of command all decide they need to also attend the briefing. These mid-level staffers and political appointees see me and they realize how junior I am…doesn't matter that I know the briefing content and ... well, this just won't do. The Deputy Secretary and the others invited to this meeting must be briefed by a more senior official. I get told to wait in the hall while my boss, Tom O'Connell, the Assistant Secretary of Defense for Special Operations, gives the brief. Which means he is basically reading off the script that I wrote. And which he had approved and agreed with and thought people further up the chain of command – like Wolfowitz and maybe even Rumsfeld, himself – ought to be made aware of.

The major point of the briefing was framed around the question: what are IEDs and what do they tell us about the bombing campaign? The answer to that question will lead you to the answer to the next, and much bigger question which was, *who is perpetrating this campaign?* And, finally, how do we develop a plan—a strategy—for fighting back. And winning.

The IED is simply the tactical manifestation of the strategic issue, which comes down to an insurgency, a resistance. Not random "dead enders" and "al Qaeda terrorists" or even, to use the silliest euphemism of them all, "violent extremists." These are the old Saddam guys, with some al Qaeda types in the mix, and they are not going peacefully. At one point in 2004, we had captured—"detained" was the euphemism—12,000 of what we were calling "militants." All but 150 were Iraqis. We weren't fighting foreign terrorists or Jihadis. We were fighting Iraqis. This was an insurgency.

The point of the briefing was to get the senior people to understand all of this and to do what would take to deal with it. We had to get past the kind of naive thinking that was summed up by President Bush's national security advisor, Condoleezza Rice, when she talked about an "old Iraq" as opposed to the new, modern, non-tribal, democratic nation we kept telling ourselves we were building.

Meanwhile, the IEDs keep going off and we were losing 80 Americans a month and a lot more Iraqis than that. And we were still looking for WMDs.

Our government has had plenty of experience in dealing with insurgencies and, as I've written, there is a counterinsurgency doctrine. But first you have to admit you have a problem and call it by its right name.

Well, that's a problem. As O'Connell learned when he was giving the briefing I wrote.

He was presenting the list of recommendations. The things I wrote about earlier: emphasis on local security, militias and police forces, standing up biometrics intelligence units to learn everything we can from the IED attacks, and rebuilding infrastructure to make the local population feel they were safe and could trust us.

And as he is presenting the list, O'Connell uses the word "insurgency."

"Now stop right there," he is told, by Doug Feith. "We are *not* using that term here in this building."

Feith is the UnderSecretary of Defense for Policy. General Tommy Franks, who was in command of the Iraq invasion, once described him as "...the fucking stupidest guy on the face of the earth."

I didn't know about that. At the time, that was a question for people above my pay grade. But I imagine that when O'Connell told me what Feith had said about how it was forbidden to use the word "insurgency" in the Pentagon, I probably felt exactly what Franks felt. And in precisely those words.

That was a long time ago. I probably felt the kind of resentment any subordinate would feel when his hard work is waved off by one of his superiors. You take it as a personal insult. First, I hadn't been allowed to give the briefing because I was too junior. Then, all my work had been waved away, like an annoying fly, because "we don't use that word around here."

What happens when you are so determined not to accept reality that you won't even call something by its name. Won't use the name—in this case "insurgency"—and are ordering people to use other words instead? Ordering them to say "dead-enders" instead of "insurgents"?

What I witnessed was the creation at the Pentagon of a sort of fantasy world where people not only denied the reality in front of their faces but created a make-believe rhetoric designed to justify their own errors of judgement (to use the kindest description) and further their own agendas and careers. The other beneficiary of this reality denial was al Qaeda, who gladly accepted the credit for the ferocity of the insurgency mounted by Saddam's former henchmen.

What replaces reality is what I call "the narrative," though I wasn't using that word at the time. It was a while before I came around to a complete understanding of what was going on and how it worked. Before, that is, I began to appreciate the reality of the Deep State. I wasn't using that phrase, either, back then.

In those days, fairly early in the Iraq war, I still believed that if I could just make the right people listen, then maybe they would *understand.* But those people, who should have known better, believed in things that were way beyond unrealistic. They were fantasies. Some of those people were sincere in their beliefs. Maybe even most of them. But there was a lot of calculation and political maneuvering. And there were people who tested the wind and went whichever way it was blowing. Human nature is what it is and it doesn't change.

Counterinsurgency is hard. But it is not expensive. It depends on ordinary soldiers and Marines, mostly equipped with inexpensive, low-tech gear, working down at street level with cops and local civilians to penetrate the insurgents' networks and provide security for the indigenous people. It isn't glamorous and like I said, it's fairly cheap.

Those were not concepts that had a lot of fans at the Pentagon where "cheap" wasn't really a virtue or even an objective. There was just so much money...*so much*, that people didn't even blink when you said you had a project—a new weapons system—that would change the battlefield and solve, say, the IED problem, and it would only cost, oh, 50 million. One hundred tops.

Cheap.

There was this sense, in the Pentagon, that a technological fix to just about any problem was out there, just waiting to be developed and deployed. You had to spend the money of course, but there was money to spend. Lots of it.

We got proposals for all sorts of new systems that were going to change the battlefield and fix our problems. It's hard to believe and hard to describe. But I literally saw 500 million-dollar projects approved after a one-slide Power Point briefing.

There was always money, it seemed, for a technological fix to a problem that needed money less than it needed brains and realistic, tough-minded, tactical thinking. We saw it all the time with the IED threat.

They're blowing up our trucks and HUMVS and shattering our convoys? Well, then, we need to find a way to up-armor the vehicles so they can survive the blast of an IED. And that wasn't going to work unless you were talking about something designed as an anti-personnel weapon. But the insurgents were building them with a lot more explosive power than that. They actually managed to build one that disabled an Abrams tank, and those are among the most heavily armored vehicles in the world. The problem with this focus on a defensive technology approach is that we were treating symptoms rather than the disease. If the passive technological approach isn't going to get it done, then how about active technological measures? That kind of thinking led to a boondoggle I actually was briefed on.

A technology company based in Virginia had the idea for a truck —something the size of a Mayflower moving van—designed to carry three huge generators in the back. The generators would power a microwave beam in front of the truck and would send out a signal that would detonate a bomb that was in the path of the truck. The truck would be at the head of a convoy of vehicles and they could follow safely along after the big truck had done its thing.

The project was interesting enough—and sounded feasible enough—to the right people in the Pentagon so a briefing was laid on. I was invited.

I was one of about 40 civilian and uniformed Pentagon people— some of them generals—sitting in a room while this PhD from the Virginia company did a fifteen or twenty-minute briefing. With slides, of course. And he finished up by saying, "We're asking for thirty million dollars to build two of them."

Nobody says anything. Not one thing about how that seems like a lot of money for two trucks. Even if they were equipped with three generators and a microwave ray gun.

Finally, I couldn't take it anymore. Even though I was one of the more junior guys in the room, with nowhere near the power to green light or shitcan the project, I raised my hand and was recognized by the PhD.

I stood up and asked my question. Respectfully.

"So when the device is detonated, how far in front of the truck is the explosion?"

The guy looked at me and answered, like he considered the question an easy one.

"Two to three meters."

Nobody says a thing. I raised my hand again.

"What is the kill radius of a 155-millimeter projectile?" I asked. Like I was just curious.

"I don't know," the guy said.

Well, I did know. I'd seen the effects.

"It's 27 meters," I said.

Still, nobody said a thing.

I sat down and thought to myself "who is driving the truck?"

The PhD's slide had a gelatin human figure driving the vehicle as part of his briefing. For many years after the briefing my staff jokingly would ask, "Who speaks for gel man?"

But the story had the usual Pentagon ending. The project was green lighted. The company from Virginia got its millions and built two of those trucks. They were shipped off to Iraq.

Where they were attacked by insurgents using RPGs. The burned-out hulks were consumed quickly by local scrap metal collectors.

Meanwhile, I couldn't get the funding we needed to stand up a task force to hunt down the bomb makers.

Denial of reality was everywhere and it ran all the way to the top in those days. One of my staff, a former SEAL with a purple heart and a degree in computer science accompanied me on a briefing. The topic was the importance of understanding the role social media was playing in the insurgency. A bureaucratic political appointee told us,

"You guys don't know what the fuck you are talking about. Social media is irrelevant." It was the year 2005. We brought up the need to supplement intelligence down below the battalion level and were told, "We are already doing that."

In one particular briefing about the need to deploy advanced targeting capabilities below the battalion level, the pushback was especially strong. A special forces warrant officer who accompanied me during the briefing jumped up in front of the room full of brass and said, "Gentlemen, I know you believe that we have all of this fantastic capability, but down below the battalion level we operate on "sneaker net." Thumb drives and CDs are how information flows." He was a man who understood the reality of the war.

When we finally did get our heads and our hands around the insurgency problem, it was in Anbar Provence where the Marines worked out a kind of tacit alliance with the Sunni tribes after the insurgents had allied too closely with the al Qaeda types and had gone too far and become too brutal. Apparently al Qaeda cooking local Iraqi children and forcing their parents to eat them was going too far. Even in Iraq.

Once the *Sunni* tribes came over, the IED attacks stopped and the insurgency went away. This was classic counter-insurgency and it was something that those of us who argued for it had been pushing for a long time. The Marines deserve a lot of credit for continuing to pursue their local tribal engagement efforts despite enormous political and policy headwinds.

The Marines leading their tribal engagement efforts ran against the narrative. The people who were bound by their own narrative and who occupied positions at the top wouldn't hear of it. At least not until everything else had failed. Earlier in the war, when the strategy of allying with the tribes had been brought up with Condoleezza

Rice, President Bush's Secretary of State, she made it clear this was not happening on her watch. Because the tribes were, in her words, "part of the old Iraq."

Yes, you might say that.

Things did finally change when it was no longer possible to keep denying reality; when the country's dissatisfaction with the war reached a point where the administration couldn't deny it any longer and the President fired Donald Rumsfeld.

I remember being on a shuttle between Crystal City and the Pentagon when I heard the news and felt this enormous sense of relief. I was a realist and knew I had no reason to believe that things were just suddenly going to get better. But I did know, pretty much to a certainty, that they couldn't get much worse.

And, in fact, they did get better. The work the Marine Corps had done in Anbar Province was followed by the "surge," and the situation in Iraq got a lot better, even if the "surge" itself received more credit for pacifying Iraq than it actually deserved. This improvement was especially noticeable in Anbar where things had been so bad that there was discussion about just abandoning the place. Seriously.

But instead, we got the Awakening. Which, like I say, got us working with the tribes and, not incidentally, paying them a lot of money. In return for the cash and for protection, they helped us find and "neutralize" the insurgents. Where it had been out of the question for an American to walk the streets of, say, Ramadi, unless it was as part of a combat patrol, it was now safe enough that you could wander around alone and unarmed. Though I wouldn't have recommended it.

The strategy of reaching out to the tribes and working with them was sound and, when you think about it, kind of obvious. A man from that province put it to me this way, "I have been Iraqi for seventy years. I have been a Muslim for 1,400 hundred years. I have been a member of the Dulaimi tribe for five thousand years." That man visited Washington around Christmas time of 2007. When he returned to Iraq, he – and several of his Marine Corps allies – were killed by a suicide bomber during a city council meeting in Karmah, Iraq on June 26, 2008.

He had been talking about *reality.* And when you make strategy, it is wise to base it on reality, not the narrative.

And when it came to ignoring reality, we had bigger problems than just those in Iraq.

THE MEMO CONTINUED Having co-opted post-modern narratives as critical points, Islamists deploy these narratives to strategically blind and then control US decision makers. This is by design and purposeful.

7

FORBIDDEN
KNOWLEDGE

Well before Donald Rumsfeld was fired as Secretary of Defense, a lot of us were troubled, and worse, by the way we were approaching what was called "the war on terror." The name itself was troubling. As I wrote earlier, "terror" is a tactic. It is not the enemy.

And then we were being told, in a pretty patronizing way, who the enemy was *not*. And that would be Islam. Which is, we were reminded over and over, a "religion of peace." The enemy was not Muslims in general, of whom there were close to two billion worldwide. If we were fighting a war on terror, then who, exactly, were the terrorists?

One answer was that they were the "extremists." That would make them al Qaeda. Members of the group behind the attack on the World Trade Center Towers. Followers of Osama bin Laden.

He and his organization were not, we were told, the *true* face of Islam.

People doing my sort of work were reminded of this, over and over, until it became almost a mantra. All together now: *Islam is not the enemy; Islam is a religion of peace.* There seemed to be a kind of fear, almost a paranoia, that people in the Pentagon wouldn't get this message. That they would succumb to the temptations of prejudice and bigotry and start thinking of all Muslims as the enemy.

There were training programs—they were almost like conscious-ness raising sessions—where Muslims with the right kind of degrees and credentials would come in and deliver lectures about the "true nature" of Islam and how it was—say it again, children: "a religion of peace."

Meanwhile, there were attacks—usually on civilians—by Muslims. Not just in Iraq but all around the world. This "war on terror" seemed to be a global conflict and the terrorists always seemed to turn out to be…Muslims.

But there was the official narrative and nobody seemed to be eager to stand up and challenge it or contradict it.

Like I say, I'd had this uneasy feeling about the narrative but didn't really know where to go with it. I was one guy doing my job in the CTTSO and trying to make the people who counted understand the nature of what was going on in Iraq.

Then, my thinking changed. Completely.

I had just gotten home from work. It was after dark and cold. A Friday in February and I was looking forward to the weekend. A couple of days off and some relief from the intensity.

The phone rang and I answered.

"May I speak to Mr. Higgins, please."

"Speaking."

The caller identified himself as a Special Agent from the FBI and that got the reaction you would expect.

I hesitated.

After a couple of seconds, I said, "What's this about? Am I in trouble or something?"

I sort of knew that I wasn't going to be read my rights and interrogated over the phone. But still …

"No. I'm calling because I'd like for you to come to a meeting tomorrow morning. In Springfield."

"What's this *meeting* about?"

I'm still on alert.

"Well, it's a series of briefings and you've been identified as someone who knows a lot of people and has influence in the counterterrorism community. You may be open to hearing a lot of what we have to say."

I thought about it for a few seconds, then said, "Okay. When and where."

"Seven o'clock," he said.

Then he read me the address and said, "See you there."

So I told my wife I had this meeting to go to the next morning. I'm up at six so I can get over to the place early and get a look at the kind of people who are showing up. About 30 or 40 cars pull into the lot and people all get out and head over to this nondescript looking warehouse. The people all sort of look like, well … like me. Government types, a lot of them in law enforcement outfits of one sort or another. I recognized one or two of them.

I followed them on into the warehouse and we all file into a classroom and take seats. The briefing starts without a lot of drama. Just, "Hey, this is who we are. We've been working counterterrorism

for five years now. We believe we have a major issue. That issue is…
we don't understand the enemy and how he operates."

I remember thinking, *Well, yeah. I guess you could call that an
"issue."*

"We don't understand Islam. Not the reality. We are in a state
of denial."

First time I'd ever heard anyone put it right out front that way.

"We're not training our guys adequately and this is causing a lot
of problems. And we want to share with you what we've found inside
our organization and ask you to share a little bit about what you're
seeing inside your own organizations. And we are going to have a
couple of folks in here today to brief us on what we are dealing with
and what we are denying."

The briefers were all frustrated by the resistance they were getting
from the top where the official line was still, "Islam is a religion of
peace."

Their response, in short, was, "No it is not."

And they proceeded to explain exactly why.

I listened and as I did, things became very clear. For me, it was
in a very real way, a "red pill moment," like that scene from the movie
"Matrix." The one with the line that goes, *You take the blue pill, the
story ends. You wake up in your bed and believe whatever you want to
believe. You take the red pill, you stay in Wonderland, and I show you
how deep the rabbit hole goes."*

That briefing opened my eyes to just how deeply into the rabbit
hole of denial we had gone. We had bought into a totally false
narrative where Islam was a "religion of peace." That it had been
"hijacked" by radicals who were responsible for 9/11 and other acts
of terrorism. And we needed Muslims to come into the Pentagon to
explain this to us. We needed to deny the evidence that *Jihad—*

"warfare to establish the religion"—was fundamental to Islam and the duty of all Muslims.

We went over some very basic, almost elementary things that had been lost, or hidden, in the effort to create this whole "religion of peace" narrative. I'll keep it simple here, because there are many places to go for more detailed treatment and because it is so easy to get deep into the weeds. In telling of this story – my story, actually – the basics are sufficient.

Islam is a religion, yes. But it is also a system of law. One which the faithful must obey and enforce. And the enforcement is ... well, call it harsh. Adulterers are still stoned to death in Muslim countries in accordance with Islamic Law.

And the Muslim adherence to, and belief in, Islamic Law (or Sharia) is not conditional. It can be pretty well summed up in this quote from the book Shari'ah: The Islamic Law by Abdur Rahman I. Doi

The Shari'ah was not revealed for limited application for a specific age. It will suit every age and time. It will remain valid and shall continue to be, till the end of this life on earth.

Nothing equivocal about that.

So, first things first: to be a Muslim means, simply and unequivocally, submission to Islamic Law. There is nothing optional about it.

Islamic Law commands Muslims to wage jihad when they are strong enough. And to continue waging jihad until the world is entirely under Islamic rule. Or, on the other hand, until they are beaten. Victory, then, or death.

It is possible to find verses in the *Qur'an* that appear to contradict these tenets. But this does not take into account the concept of "abrogation," which holds that the later pronouncements of Muhammed—received directly from Allah—abrogated any that came earlier and were contradictory. So, if something that Allah had spoken to Muhammed, in his early years, about the brotherhood of man was in conflict with, say, the verses cited above, then the later verses were the law. It also doesn't take into account the "perfect example" of Muhammad himself, which serves as the exemplar for all Muslims for all times.

I spent a full year, later on, researching Islam to produce a master's thesis for war college. I have a fairly deep and even technical understanding of Islam now. But when I went into that room, for that "Red Pill" briefing, I was naive, like most Americans.

Now, someone reading this story might reasonably ask, "Why was it necessary to go off-site on a weekend to this briefing? Why was it done in such…well, *clandestine* fashion?

And the answer is that while the attendees and briefers were serious people, what they had to say was not taken seriously by powerful people inside the Pentagon and the FBI and every other element of the government that had anything to do with our "war on terror."

It has been more than ten years, but I can still remember that briefing and how I felt as I sat there listening to what the briefers were telling us. About jihad. Islamic law. The Muslim Brotherhood. The FBI briefers knew a lot about the Holy Land Foundation case in Texas in which the FBI had infiltrated and exposed a Muslim Brotherhood operation that was described as the largest terrorist fundraising operation in U.S. history.

I knew a little about the Muslim Brotherhood but I had no idea of its reach or its tenacity. I was still in that place where most Americans were. Islam is just another religion. There are people who are Muslims in the same way that I'm a Catholic and someone else is a Baptist. The American way of thinking about these things, you know.

That guy who belongs to the Muslim Brotherhood and is down in Texas raising illegal cash for Hamas? When he looks at me, he doesn't see a Catholic or a Christian or something equivalent. To him, I'm not just somebody who buys into a different way of worshiping God. What he sees, and thinks, is...*infidel.*

So much of my thinking changed during and after that briefing that it would have been impossible to go back even if I had wanted to. I understood how it could happen that a few days after the 9/11 attacks, President George Bush could deliver a speech from the Washington DC Islamic Center in which he called Islam "a religion of peace" and did it with several Muslim men standing beside him. One of them, an American citizen named Abdul Rahman al-Amoudi, is now in federal prison. The reason—he was al Qaeda.

While I was outraged, I was not surprised when Major Nidal M. Hasan killed 13 people, mostly soldiers, and wounded another 31, at Fort Hood, Texas, in November 2009. Hasan was an Army psychiatrist who had been briefing people—in the Pentagon—that, as a Muslim, he could not go to Afghanistan or Iraq to wage war against, and kill, his fellow Muslims. He had made it just about as clear as he could that he was not a loyal American soldier. He warned that ordering him to deploy would result in "adverse consequences." Consequences demanded by Islamic law. The FBI had even listened in on conversations between Major Hasan and Anwar al-Awaki in Yemen where he was doing al Qaeda's work until the drone strike that killed him.

Astonishingly, there were news accounts of the shooting where the question of motive was raised. *Why* did Hasan do this? Was he *really* a terrorist? Or just emotionally disturbed?

Could Islam have had something to do with it?

Did he kill those people because he was a *jihadist* doing what *jihadists* are called to do? Namely, wage *jihad.* Kill infidels. Was it relevant and important that he was shouting *Allah Akbar* before he opened up with his FN® pistol?

I wasn't asking that kind of foolish question. I *knew.* The Obama Administration said it was "workplace violence." My ass. I had known since that "red pill briefing."

But if I wasn't surprised, I was certainly angry at the pervasive effort not to see that multiculturalism is literally killing us. This willful ignorance and denial peaked when Army Chief of Staff General George Casey said of the Fort Hood attack, "Our diversity, not only in our Army, but in our country, is a strength. And as horrific as this tragedy was, if our diversity becomes a casualty, I think that's worse."

By the time of the Hassan killings and Casey's utterly feckless response, I began to examine the world I lived and worked in, something that people would eventually describe as "the Deep State." The phrase has a sinister sound and there is a certain super- ficial validity to that. But the phrase implies that government and Wash- ington are more conspiratorial than they really are. In a lot of ways, the Deep State operates right out in the open.

Washington and the government run on the basic human impulses, self-interest being paramount. And loyalty to the institu- tions to which someone belongs. If you work for the FBI your insti- tutional loyalty is to the Bureau. If you work for the Pentagon, then your institutional loyalty is to the Pentagon. When Donald Rumsfeld says he doesn't want to hear the word "insurgency" used inside those five sets of walls, and you work in the Pentagon, then you listen and you make sure the word "insurgency" never passes your lips.

You don't think of yourself as someone who is doing something wrong or denying the truth. And you sort of internalize what I think of as "the narrative." It isn't based on fact, of course. It is a fiction. But it is the fiction that your institutional loyalty ensures, and self-interest demands.

When Bush said, "Islam is a religion of peace," he set the narrative and you could not deviate from it, even as you're watching jihadists literally saw off people's heads with carving knives and chanting from the Quran as they did it.

So that's how you have a war, like Iraq or Afghanistan where we are rapidly approaching our 20th anniversary of futile combat. Last week, as I write, an EOD guy, 23 years old, married with a baby on the way, was killed there. For what?

That kid's not going to have a dad. Because the people who could have kept him from ever going there are more loyal to the Deep State narrative than they are to him, their countryman.

THE MEMO CONTINUED Because the hard left is aligned with Islamist organizations at local (ANTIFA working with Muslim Brotherhood doing business as MSA and CAIR), national (ACLU and BLM working with CAIR and MPAC) and international levels (OIC working with OSCE and the UN), recognition must given to the fact that they seamlessly interoperate at the narrative level as well.

8

TRENCH WARFARE:
BUREAUCRAT STYLE

When I returned, after the red pill briefing, to my job with CTTSO, I not only saw things differently, but began doing what I could to make others see what I now saw. And of course, this created friction. I made enemies.

The Pentagon is an enormous bureaucracy where the turf wars never end. People fight for their programs and their policies and that is to be expected. But there was something new and dangerous in play in those years after the 9/11 attacks. The fights over whether to spend money on submarines or aircraft carriers, conventional infantry and armor units or special forces, close air support aircraft or supersonic fighter/bombers ... those fights went on and, as long as there is a Pentagon, they probably will. Everybody sees his program or service branch as critical and essential and fights for it.

But what was different in those years was that there was a kind of ideological infiltration of the Pentagon. People were pushing a politically correct narrative and they were not doing it in the manner of a college debate club.

Early in 2008, they went after a man named Steve Coughlin, who knows as much about Islam and Islamic law as anyone. Coughlin was briefing people in the Pentagon all the way up to the Joint Chiefs and he was effective. Which is understandable since he told the truth. And this, of course, made him a target. Someone who needed to be taken out. And was.

The people who did it tried to make it look like routine administrative stuff. Their line was that Coughlin had fulfilled the terms and dates of his contract and it was simply not renewed. All of that is a euphemistic way of saying he was fired.

Coughlin had actually been set up by a suspected Muslim Brother, who baited Steve into a shouting match at a meeting and then went to his protector, Gordon England, to complain.

You didn't offend a Muslim who was under the protection of a Deputy Secretary of Defense and stay around. But there were those of us—not many, unfortunately—who were willing to fight back. After the Red Pill meeting, I was one of them.

We knew that this particular Muslim Brother was working on "outreach" to Muslim groups, including the Islamic Society of North America, which was straight-up Muslim Brotherhood, which was decidedly *not* a secular organization like its defenders were claiming. The Muslim Brotherhood's openly stated goal is the restoration of the Caliphate under the rule of Islamic law.

Worldwide.

My boss and I worked to keep Coughlin around and we got Vice-President Cheney's office behind us. It took a few months, but we got it done and Coughlin had a new contract, this time with the CTTSO. It was a win, but a small one. And we were, obviously, playing defense.

We also made sure people in the media learned about the Muslim Brother and his sketchy biography. He claimed he'd experienced an Israeli bombing of his family's neighborhood in Cairo when he was young but there are no records to support this. There was no bombing of civilian neighborhoods in Cairo by Israeli airplanes, ever. Likewise, his claim of having survived the sinking of a cargo ship after it was torpedoed by the Israelis. No journalist was ever able to confirm such an action, much less that this Muslim Brother spent two days in the water before he was rescued.

It wasn't hard, however, to establish that he had negative feelings about Israel. In a master's thesis written for the Naval Postgraduate School in Monterey, Calif, the Muslim Brother described what he called, "Israeli activities which have detrimentally affected U.S. objectives but which have continued with impunity," and he went on to generally decry the influence of Jews on American foreign policy.

This is who he was. He had influence and it was clear where his sympathies lie. As a result of the Muslim Brotherhood's outreach efforts, Muslim prayer ceremonies were conducted in a chapel in the Pentagon that was only a few feet from the point where the plane struck the building on 9/11. In fact, the DoD's entire Muslim chaplain corps was established by a top al Qaeda fundraiser who was ultimately sentenced to 23 years in jail. What kind of Muslim chaplains do you think he chose for this program? Were any of them removed after we found out it was al Qaeda choosing our chaplains? You already know the answer.

And if that's not enough, al Qaeda cleric Anwar al-Awlaki, who was eventually killed in a US drone strike, attended lunches in the Pentagon's Navy dining facility, and senior defense department officials deferred to these hostile influence agents in the course of their strategic decision-making processes.

So that was the mood and the atmosphere around the Pentagon. And in other parts of the defense establishment. The Brotherhood had a strong presence, for instance, at West Point of all places. And there was a program that pushed for more and more Muslim chaplains in all the services. It sometimes seemed like the Defense Department was more concerned about the feelings of Muslims than it was interested in fighting what were called, inevitably, "extremists."

Which might have been an accurate description, as far as it went. But being "extremists" did not make them rare or unusual. The Brotherhood's politics are certainly "extreme," their tactics less violent perhaps, but in terms of numbers and influence, it is not a fringe group. Far from it, as the world learned during the uprisings around the mid-East, known as the "Arab Spring."

But that came later during the Obama years, which were even worse than the Bush years for willing disbelief of the truth that was right there, in front of everyone's eyes.

For example, there was evidence that was entered in a 2008 trial that dealt with the Holy Land Foundation. The FBI found a document in the home of Ismael Elbarasse, a founder of a mosque in Falls Church, Virginia and a member of something called the "Palestine Committee," which had been created by the Brotherhood. Its mission was to support Hamas in the United States. Here are some excerpts from that document:

> * Enablement of Islam in North America, meaning: estab-
> lishing an effective and a stable Islamic Movement led by
> the Muslim Brotherhood

* the Movement must plan and struggle to obtain "the keys" and the tools of this process in carry out [sic] this grand mission as a 'Civilization Jihadist' responsibility.

* *The Ikhwan [Muslim Brotherhood] must understand that their work in America is a kind of grand jihad in eliminating and destroying the Western civilization from within and* **"sabotaging" its miserable house by their hands** *and the hands of the believers… We must possess a mastery of the art of "coalitions," the art of "absorption,"and the principles of "cooperation."*

By their own hands! The Muslim Brotherhood strategy was to get our leadership to impose the Muslim Brotherhood's wishes upon us. Made sense. Saw it everyday.

There were a few people in the Pentagon who were willing to recognize the truth about the Brotherhood and were pushing back. Those who had not taken the blue "denial" pill. People like Coughlin and…well, me. But there were not enough of us. We were outranked and outnumbered.

Every now and then we would win one. Like getting Coughlin back. But we were playing defense the whole way. We always felt outnumbered. We were marginalized through systemic labeling and slander. "Conspiracy theorist" was their favorite.

And that was during the Bush administration.

After Obama was elected, it got worse.

Just days after the election, they came after me personally. And it didn't take the typical form of bureaucratic subversion and backbiting. They weren't firing blanks any longer. It was live rounds in the form of an Inspector General (IG) investigation that was opened on me and a project I'd been running. It could have ended my career, at the very least, and resulted in criminal charges and jail time at worst. It was meant to ruin me and it was clearly payback.

It was also bullshit.

Here is the story:

I'd had some people working on a project in Africa and they were past the dates of their contract. I was working to get them renewed and the paperwork backdated. Bureaucratic stuff. Dotted lines and checked boxes. It happened all the time. Things were always getting stranded in the labyrinth of paperwork. People always had more important things to do and the red tape could wait

Well, these guys who were working for me were all former special forces and intelligence types and they didn't miss much. The mission had them researching the man-hunting techniques of non-state actors. Say, for example, you owe the Russian mob a lot of money. How would the Russian mob find you and get its money and take whatever other measures it considered appropriate?

During the time while my guys were in contract limbo, but still in the field, and working with some intelligence people from a country in East Africa, they came across a piece of very high value intelligence. Something that would pinpoint the location of one of our HVTs. High Value Targets.

They got this information back to me and I got it into the system and down to Fort Bragg through the proper channels. I wasn't real worried about whether these guys were actually under contract or on the payroll when I did this. I figured getting that information into the right hands and making sure action was taken might just be a little more important than checking all the right paperwork boxes.

So, there was an op launched on the basis of that information and a missile strike took out that HVT. It made the front page of the *New York Times*. Above the fold.

It also resulted in my being investigated by the IG for running a rogue op with people who were not, technically, under contract. So, now, I was a target. Like they say, no good deed goes unpunished.

I was now...what? Not an outcast, exactly. But radioactive, certainly. And not as effective as I needed to be. Which was maybe the point. As long as I was being investigated and under a cloud, I was going to be a problem for the CTTSO and for my boss.

So, my boss, Ed McCallum said, "We need to get you someplace where you aren't a big shiny target." And he detailed me over to the National Defense University. I remembered, then, how he'd told me when I first went to work for him, "You'll find out, pretty soon, that there is no light at the top."

I hadn't quite understood at the time, but I did now.

THE MEMO CONTINUED Academia has served as a principle counter-state node for some time and remains a key conduit for creating future adherents to cultural Marxist narratives and their derivative worldview.

9

A SABBATICAL
... OF SORTS

S o I was out of action. It had happened to Coughlin and now it had happened to me.

While I was no longer on the front lines when it came to counterterrorism, I was still in game. And though I might have had reason to feel like I had been exiled, this was not Russia and the National Defense University was certainly not Siberia.

The NDU is located at Fort McNair, an old Army base—the third oldest, in fact—that is still operational. The building where I attended my classes was called Lincoln Hall and it was handsomely built in the neo-classical style. The structure was both formidable and beautiful and it looked out on the base's tennis courts, which were built upon the grounds where the gallows used to execute conspirators in the plot to assassinate Abraham Lincoln had once been erected. The Potomac river sparkles in the distance.

If you had to be exiled, there were worse places you could be sent.

And worse ways that I could have spent the time.

There are several courses of study that are taught at the National Defense University and a number of people who have studied there have gone on to bigger things. This includes, especially, military people who have achieved high flag rank and, many of them, a place in history. Among them, Colin Powell, Peter Pace, and many others. There were numerous representatives from other government agencies as well. Although I did not know him personally, one of my classmates was Ambassador Christopher Stevens, who would later lose his life in Benghazi, Libya.

It was good duty then. And since my course of study was counterterrorism, I was comfortable being there and I threw myself into the work. I was up at five so I could leave the house early and beat the traffic. I hit the gym every day. Classes started at eight and I was at Ft. McNair until late afternoon. There was homework and I was required to write a thesis in order to graduate.

There were two especially interesting aspects to my time at the war college. First, there were a lot of foreign students in the course and many of them were from countries where counterterrorism wasn't some abstract, academic concept or course of study. It was the reality of their country's life. We had students from India, Afghanistan, Thailand, Columbia, and others. They were familiar, first hand, with the realities of counterterrorism as well as experts in the concepts and the theory. It was, in short, a true and first-rate education into theory and practice.

I ate it up. And I didn't come to the proceedings empty handed. My exposure to the subject of counterterrorism had been my time in Iraq and those years dealing with the threat of IEDs and working with organizations like the British SAS and the Israeli Shin Bet. I had done my own reading, and a lot of it, but at the college it was structured and I was required to write papers and defend my conclusions. It was...shall we say, *bracing*.

And, then, a lot of those foreign students were Muslims. It had been a couple of years, now, since my "red pill" meeting and I had learned a lot more about Islam through self-study. The Muslims among my fellow students recognized, when we talked, that I was knowledgeable about Islam and this led to an interesting dynamic. The majority of these people were not fanatics. They didn't buy into bin Ladin. So we could talk. But they knew they couldn't bullshit me about Islamic law and they knew that I understood the requirement of Islam that no true Muslim could speak truthfully to an infidel about his faith. Still, we talked frankly...up to a point.

We did have one student, he was a Colonel from Pakistan, who was a radical Muslim and tried to disguise it. At least most of the time. But I saw through it and some of the Muslim students realized that I did. This gave me a little more status in their eyes.

The Pakistani Colonel accompanied the entire class on a trip to U.S. Special Operations Command (USSOCOM) in Tampa, FL. During one of the briefings by the command's staff, a senior US flag officer was briefing about nationalism and used Pakistan as an illustrative example. The Pakistani Colonel stood up in the middle of the briefing, enraged, ranting about Pakistan being a Muslim country, and shouting down the general. He then stormed out of the conference room.

I believe that guy was a member of the Pakistani secret services and that he was on a mission. None of the senior Pakistani officers present said a word. It would be interesting to know what he reported when he went back to his country after spending a year of studying among people who would soon be leading the United States military and who he might be facing in combat one day.

I completed a one-year course at war college. I read the books. I attended the lectures. Wrote the papers and my thesis. Graduated with a master's degree in national security studies and then, stayed on for another year as faculty. I was given the lofty title of Chair for Special Operations and Low Intensity Conflict. In my second year, I spent a lot of time and study on Islam and wrote several papers.

One very important take away from these two years at NDU was a deep appreciation for Eastern warfighting strategies and concepts. Americans, myself included, tended to base their understanding of warfare on Western concepts. However, a focus on eastern and other non-Western concepts of warfare opened my eyes to a whole new level of understanding and appreciation of national security strategy. One that would be important later. When it would be needed here. At home.

The concept of political warfare—particularly as understood by Mao Tse Tung—requires the examination of social/political movements into national security contexts.

One of my professors, Tom Marks, describes Maoist political warfare in five lines of effort: violence, non-violence, alliances, sanctuaries (including cyber), and political warfare or massline. The core of this strategic approach is the synchronizing of all lines of effort into the political warfare line of effort, with the explicit purpose of growing a **political movement**. It's what we're seeing here across the progressive democrat spectrum – from "community organizers" to AntiFa. This increasing mobilization, or massing, enables what may begin as a small group of committed believers to acquire a greater and greater share of political power.

I suppose you could say that since even before 9/11, I had been engaged in the study of counterterrorism. It had, in a way, been the focus of my life, beginning at just about the most practical and basic level. With, that is, the essential weapon of the terrorists, the IED. I had studied IEDs and the people who built and deployed them. It was counterterrorism at street level.

From there, I had moved gradually from the tactical to the operational. At CTTSO, I had been working more and more on tactical problems and solutions. We were interested in getting inside of terrorists networks and taking them down, and on solutions that might come under the heading of "counterinsurgency."

Then, when I went over to the National Defense University, it was a move from the tactics to the strategy of counterterrorism. Which takes you into the realm of...politics.

It was becoming clear to me that no amount of skillful, ingenious engineering and no degree of tactical proficiency was going to get us to a win in what was still being called the "war on terror," if we could not think strategically and clearly. And the fact that we couldn't call the enemy by his name was proof, to me, that we still could not win. "Radical extremism," was not the enemy any more than "workplace violence" was responsible for the Fort Hood massacre.

At the end of my two years at the National Defense University, I had this sense that there was a next step out there that would take me ... well, who knew where? But I would find out.

But first, there was that IG investigation.

It had continued through my time at the National Defense University and that can be the way with these things. Especially when they are not really about any violation or infraction but are designed to immobilize someone who is seen as a threat to the prevailing narrative. Someone, that is, who is not a good team player. Who is working his own agenda. Doesn't make any difference if the agenda is right or not. The problem is that the agenda does not conform to the narrative. So the longer they drag it out, the better for them. Because clearing you, or even just giving you a slap on the wrist, means you go back to work and causing problems. Because you are "not a team player" and so on and so forth.

But while I may have been more or less exiled from the Pentagon, I was still trying to get some exposure for what I consider the reality of things in Iraq with the misnamed "war on terror." With the "Islam is a religion of peace" delusion.

This is Washington and what people who have never been creatures of "the swamp" or worked for the Deep State can't fully appreciate is how much it is a place and a culture that depends on networking. In Washington, it is all about contacts and who you know and who can help you advance whatever agenda it is you are pushing. It is a town full of lobbyists, lawyers, journalists, politicians, bureaucrats, and spies. The currency is influence via access and reputation. And to a much lesser degree than in, say, New York ... money. The Director of the CIA is an enormously powerful and important Washington player and barely part of the upper middle class when it comes to money and economic status. In New York, on what he gets paid, he would have the power and influence of ... well, maybe a truck driver or construction worker.

People in Washington like influence and power and they network with other people who do, as well, and who can help them advance their agenda. It sounds sinister and conspiratorial and it sometimes can be. But most of the time, it is just human beings acting in a way that blends idealism and self-interest. That is, in other words ... *political.*

I had been moving into that world more and more. Moving from being strictly a tech and systems guy into someone who thought and cared more about policy. I had started in Washington as a guy who checked the briefcases and bags of congressmen and senators when they arrived at the White House for meetings and briefings, into a guy who went up to Capitol Hill to brief Congressmen and Senators on what I thought they ought to know about counterterrorism and other policy issues.

This was, I suppose, sort of inevitable. Somebody you know, who shares your views, says to someone who works on the Hill, "Hey, there's this guy over at the Pentagon. He knows the IED thing cold, you ought to get him into your boss's office to do a briefing."

So you are invited up to the Hill and you do the briefing and then you go out for drinks afterwards with some of the senior staff. And they introduce you to other people on the Hill. Or in the media. You are networking and you know people and they know you. And pretty soon, you are a player in the never-ending game of Washington politics.

I wasn't particularly partisan about it. I grew up in a blue-collar Boston family where, until Reagan, you would have drunk poison before you voted for a Republican. I didn't like the way Republicans were – and are – willing to sell out working people to advance the agenda of the Chamber of Commerce people and the country club crowd. People like ... oh, George W. Bush. Or Mitt Romney. Or Paul Ryan. The kind of people who couldn't abide Donald Trump or his policy positions and who looked down their noses at people out in the forgotten parts of the country, beyond Washington, who supported Trump because he shared their views about ... well, about America.

So when I went up to the Hill, I briefed both Republicans and Democrats. Didn't make any difference to me. I briefed John McCain and I briefed Joe Lieberman. Among others.

McCain and I had some pretty testy exchanges. He was a very influential presence on the Senate Armed Services Committee because of his military background and he stayed involved in the kind of issues those of us in the Pentagon worked on and cared about. This included numerous projects of mine over the years. So I was in his office a few times to brief him and a couple of times, things got pretty heated. I'd say something like, "Look, sir, you know, you're missing this," and he would get very stern and aggravated. But I'd stick to my guns.

There was an occasion, during the Obama presidency, when I went up to the Hill to brief McCain on some of what we were seeing inside the Arab Spring and the ascendency of Morsi. Some of what I briefed him on came straight from guys I knew on the ground over in Egypt. And McCain just did not want to hear it. He said something about how, "These people are fighting for freedom."

Which was BS, of course. Every guerrilla fighter or revolutionary says he is a "freedom fighter." Castro's people were "freedom fighters." The Bolsheviks were "freedom fighters." And the Muslim Brotherhood people who were the drivers of the Arab Spring claimed they were "freedom fighters."

In my conversation with McCain, I brought up Sayyid Qutb's book, "Milestones," which was the intellectual foundation of the Arab Spring uprisings in the same way that say, the Communist Manifesto was for the Russian Revolution. And Qutb was very clear in what he wrote about jihad. As one writer put it, he urged Muslims to separate themselves "from mainstream society and engage in violent jihad." This was to force submission, all over the world, to Allah.

Qutb writings and legacy, by the way, are also foundational to the Muslim Brotherhood and al Qaeda.

McCain wasn't interested. I couldn't be talking about Morsi, because, "You know, I've met this guy, and he's okay."

So you reach a point where you decide the guy just doesn't have a very firm grip on the nature of Islam or at least no interest in hearing from you about it. This becomes exceedingly clear when he tells you, "You don't know what you are talking about."

I never raised my voice, or anything, but I made it pretty clear that I didn't agree with him so he just eventually stood up and left the room.

I remember thinking when I walked out of his office, "Boy, I'm glad that guy did not become President."

But there were other people who I met—and networked with—who did listen and who did think the way I did and were concerned the way I was. This was especially true during the Obama years and after I was cleared by the IG investigation. My offense was finally ruled to be unorthodox for sure, but administrative. The equivalent of putting paperwork in the wrong file or something on that order. I was officially censured for my failure of administrative oversight, but I was unofficially congratulated and thanked.

Typical.

THE MEMO CONTINUED The democratic leadership has been a counter-state enabler that executes, sustains, and protects cultural Marxist programs of action and facilitates the relentless expansion of the Deep State.

10

THE OBAMA YEARS: FROM BAD TO WORSE

Obama and his people didn't seem to like the U.S. military except when it was good for a photo op. They didn't like the war on terror. They wanted to patch things up with Iran and destabilize the secular, autocratically ruled countries in the mid-East in favor of more Islamist rule. This was the subject of a secret presidential study. In the eyes of the Obama administration, if the Muslim Brotherhood's influence in the middle-east increased and that of the dictators like Gaddafi declined, then that would be a *good* thing.

The danger was unmistakable to anyone who was looking and understood the Muslim Brotherhood. Which didn't appear to include anyone in the senior foreign policy ranks of the Obama administration. Those people seemed totally surprised by what came to be called "The Arab Spring." In hindsight, I am not so sure that there was much surprise.

In late 2010, mobs took to the streets. First in Oman, then Yemen. Then Egypt, Syria, and Morocco. The presidents of Tunisia and Egypt were forced from office. A Muslim Brotherhood influenced coup took down Mobarik in Egypt and replaced him with Morsi. And it threatened to spread to the rest of the middle-East and advance, like nothing else ever had, the Brotherhood's goal of a new caliphate.

In Libya, Gaddafi was eventually overthrown and killed. Secretary of State, Hillary Clinton, was especially thrilled by this and said, sort of gleefully, "We came; we saw; he died."

But, of course, there was more to it. Libya descended into a state of anarchy, one result of which was the attack on the U.S. facility in Benghazi during which the U.S. Ambassador, Christopher Stevens was killed, along with another State Department official and two contractors who were there for security.

No rescue team was sent to help them.

Explicit orders were issued not to intervene. Commanders bristled and at least two were relieved.

Disgraceful.

What happened at that annex that caused the Obama administration to leave a US Ambassador and his colleagues to fend for themselves while under attack? Why was the State Department not prepared on the eleventh anniversary of the attacks on the Twin Towers and Pentagon?

Clinton and the rest of the administration tried to peddle a story that the attack was some kind of spontaneous uprising of people indignant about the release, in the U.S., of an anti-Muslim video.

Susan Rice went on every Sunday morning political talk show to make this case. But it was bullshit and they knew it. But to them, the narrative was more important than the truth. And it was a heck of a truth.

Among the other consequences of the policies outlined in an administration policy document were the destabilization and subsequent near-destruction of Syria and the rise of ISIS.

Not bad for a single Presidential paper. The bureaucratic language of the document—which is still classified—is benign enough. I know because I have seen it. But the core message and the effects are dramatic and revolutionary. It is a shocking document that places the USA firmly behind the Arab Spring and the subsequent rise of ISIS.

What Obama was doing in the realm of foreign policy spilled over into his feelings about, and relations with, the U.S. military.

Obama had, of course, never served. In fact, it would have been hard to find anyone in his senior staff who had. The administration was heavy with Ivy League theorists and short on guys who had been out where policy meets reality and gotten dirty. Or bloody.

And Obama wanted his kind of senior officers. That would be the kind who would say the sort of thing that General Casey had said after the Fort Hood shootings that left 13 dead and more than 30 wounded. Who would go along with calling it an episode of "workplace violence" and not "terrorism," which it plainly was, as anyone not blinded by the brilliance of PC could see.

If you didn't toe that kind of line and buy in to the narrative, then you were gone. Passed over for promotion, retired early, given dead end assignments. This wasn't about tactics, strategy or, even, weapon systems and procurement. It wasn't Truman/MacArthur or Lincoln/McClellan. It was PC and ideology.

You had things like the dismissal of Gen. Carter Ham who disagreed with orders _not_ to launch a rescue mission in response to the Sept. 11, 2012 attack on the U.S. mission in Benghazi.

And the relief of Rear Adm. Chuck Gaouette as commander of the John C. Stennis Carrier Strike Group because he was said to have disobeyed orders by sending his forces to assist General Ham in a rescue at Benghazi.

Those were just the high profile, public examples. There were dozens of others. Some for one specious "cause" or another. Some for no given reason. Which, to my thinking, meant it all came down to two things:

"Political Correctness" and corruption.

You got more and more senior officers – officers of all ranks, actually – who were good at testing the winds and at mouthing the PC platitudes. They might not be "Chesty" Puller or "Bull" Halsey or George Patton but they could, by God, say things like what I actually heard one of them say.

"The greatest challenge facing the American military is dealing with climate change."

To which one can only think, "God help us."

So that was the mood of the Pentagon during the time I was away at war college and the subject of that IG investigation and all through the Obama years. Frustrating times, needless to say. But I was more concerned for the havoc and the disruptions that were being caused by the Obama administration than I was for myself. I don't say that to come off as brave and selfless, but because I'd known that my supposed offenses were bullshit designed to serve two purposes.

First, to put a scare into me and, second, to shut me down.

I'd be lying if I said I wasn't a little nervous when I first learned about the investigation. There is a reason that everyone knows what the word "Kafkaesque" means, whether or not they have read *The Trial*. I mean, I suppose if they had really wanted to get me, maybe they could have. But the truth is, people whose job is to do those investigations aren't that good. They aren't the old KGB or the Stasi. They have a lot of resources and all the time in the world so they can keep you tied up in knots for a long time but … well, when it comes down to it, they are American bureaucrats. This is scary enough, I suppose, in its own way. What you learn, after you have been in Washington and served in the Deep State long enough, is that it is more about people protecting their posteriors than projecting real power. They didn't necessarily want me in jail. They just wanted me gone.

So after Obama was re-elected in 2012, I left government service. For the private sector. But before I left, there was one last assignment after I had completed war college.

AND THE MEMO CONTINUED Political correctness is a weapon against reason and critical thinking. This weapon functions as the enforcement mechanism of diversity narratives that seek to implement cultural Marxism.

11

EXFILTRATION: LEAVING LEVIATHAN

My old billet at CTTSO had been there and waiting for me when I finished at the National Defense University. And there was a new project. There was never a shortage of projects in the world of counterterrorism back then. I threw myself into this one.

There had been a request from Special Operations Command, and a captain from SEAL Team Six, to stand up a special project that needed some help from somebody who had a background in non-traditional counterterrorism capabilities and understood the acquisition and contracting side of things. Knew, that is, how to execute projects and programs. So, I was detailed to support Captain "Pete" at an office that became known as Special Operations Command National Capital Region.

When we started, it was literally just the two of us—Pete and me—and we ended up getting an office in Crystal City. We ran the project out of there until it closed shop early in 2013.

There is a lot about the project that is still classified but the basics come down to this:

Special Operations Command had people all over the world and in these various places that they were deployed, they would have an ongoing series of contacts with various local vendors, businesses and so forth. What we wanted to do was put in place an information sharing architecture that would give us access to friendly infrastructures in an operation. Say, for example, a US company's oil platform off the coast of Algeria comes under attack and we have a hostage situation with 50 American oil workers being held captive by an al Qaeda affiliate.

We need to know who had local commercial naval assets available that would not look like they were military. Who had local airports that could handle a C-130 landing? Who had these kind of infrastructure assets which did not belong to the US or some foreign government but would be available and useful in a rescue mission?

That's about as opaque and descriptive as I can make it. It will have to do.

This project had Pete and me dealing a lot with private sector actors. The kind of people, for instance, who were CEOs of international corporations that had assets, to include human assets, that might be seized and held hostage in a terrorist situation.

There was one occasion I remember, in New York, where Pete and I met with several billionaires, including Hank Greenberg from AIG. They were all more than willing to assist us in developing out our networks.

We were also looking at the technological side of things. Take that oil platform I used as an example. If it had been seized and we wanted to take it back, and it has cameras, then how do we get those data feeds and give a Navy strike team access to them?

There was a lot of that sort of thing and it was a good project until the House Appropriations Committee shut it down in early 2013 because it didn't approve of the way that SOCOM had paid for it.

At that point, I basically got sent back to CTTSO, which had been a hostile environment for me when I left three-and-a-half or four years earlier. Now that Obama had been re-elected...well, it was even worse.

The politically correct, bureaucratic operators were everywhere and I was on all their lists. They made it their mission to block me from being able to really do anything. It was bureaucrat prison. *Dilbert* on steroids.

So that was frustrating. Especially after having worked on projects where I'd been given my reins and lots of room to run. And then, at the time, I was going through a tough divorce.

So it seemed like a good time to pull the plug and get completely out of the government.

That didn't mean, however, leaving counterterrorism, which had been my world for more than seventeen years. It is a small world and, in a way, very parochial. It consists mostly of insiders and you start to feel like the only people who get it, who *understand*, are the other people who, like you, live in that world.

I've written earlier about how in Iraq, in 2003, the intelligence community had a bar at their compound called the HVT Bar—the High-Value Target Bar. It was a dingy, ratty little place where people would go to unwind and tell war stories and one night when I'm there, I go outside to smoke a cigarette.

While I'm still outside, this other guy comes out to smoke and naturally we start talking. I ask him what he's been doing and he tells me. He asks me what I've been doing and I tell him. It's just two guys bullshitting, you know. Telling war stories, and trying to make them interesting, at least. Or, better than that … funny.

Eventually, we go back inside the bar and that's that. Never got the guy's name. Then ten years later, I get back from a flight overseas, England or somewhere, and I get off the plane at Dulles Airport and I'm standing out front having a cigarette and who walks up next to me?

"Hey man," he says, "good to see you. Where did you run for the past 10 years?"

It was coincidence, of course. But it also confirms something someone said to me once, "You know, it's always the same 500 guys. The soldiers come and go, and the generals come and go, but there is a core group—a lot of them contractors, some of them government—that always shows up in these fights."

That's absolutely true. And it gets to where that is the only world you know and you can't imagine living in another one.

So while I left the government, I stayed in that world and I ended up going to work for a company I had dealt with while I was reporting for SOCOM. I stayed in DC, kept my security clearances and all that, so my professional life didn't change that much.

The other parts, however, were in … well, not chaos, exactly, but under some strain. There was the divorce and that was some heavy weather. And I had been doing this counterterrorism without recognizing the toll. It was stressful. And the pressure had taken different forms and sometimes you don't recognize it until later.

In late 2010, maybe early 2011, for instance, I was accused, in an official and threatening way, of being a racist, xenophobe, and a bigot. It started with an army private named Naser Abdo who went on Al Jazeera with a video in which he's making all these statements that to the normal ear just sounded like he was complaining about life in the U.S. Army and how he wished it were more multi-cultural and all that sort of stuff. It could be passed off as just the usual soldier bitching but what I and a few others realized was ... this guy was threatening to attack Americans just like Major Hassan had done at Fort Hood.

On Al Jazeera.

In his army uniform.

He was, straight up, a traitor.

I sent an email, through two channels. First, to the appropriate Pentagon office asking, "Who is this guy and why is he on television and who is his commander and why isn't he doing something about it? And, oh, by the way, this guy is threatening an attack." Second, to an email distro list I participated on that included some very influential national security people.

There was never any official response. The distro list response that came back basically said I was not just wrong, but I was making this stuff up because I was a racist and I should be fired for saying it.

Well, about four months after that e-mail exchange, then-specialist Abdo was arrested at Fort Hood, where he had gone to do another terrorist attack. An alert gun store owner caught on to him, and he is now in Colorado at the supermax prison.

The point of that story is that, unless you know Islam and you know what people like that are talking about—where, you might say, they are "coming from"—you can't understand what they are actually saying. What they are communicating to you. And you won't know it even when they are telling you right to your face that they are going to kill you.

But being right isn't necessarily easy. And there were other episodes and battles that were not quite so dramatic, but they all came with their price.

During this time, a friend of mine, who was the former Alpha Squadron Commander of Delta Force, convinced me to go through this program called Operation Restore Warrior or ORW. His basic pitch was, "Look, I'm not saying you have PTSD, I'm just saying that when you are dealing with this stuff all the time—and it's heavy stuff—it just wears on your soul. You need to get yourself right with God, you need to kind of get a better picture of where things are in this big temporal battle we're all fighting inside the big spiritual battle we're also fighting."

I had been raised Catholic. Even went to a Catholic high school. I didn't hate the church, but felt very let down by their fixation on money and hierarchy and their unwillingness to fight against government social engineering. So I went through.

ORW is a five-day program founded by Delta Force veterans for veterans and for men who deal with war. Veterans, cops, FBI agents and CIA guys go through this program. It's a Christian-based program for men only and it put the various experiences, frustrations, battles, losses, and victories, all into context. It really made me a much better father and it opened my eyes to the nature of the battle of good versus evil that's going on all around us all the time.

What you do is…you go off on a retreat where you're not allowed to have any outside contact with the world—no television, no radios, no phones, no nothing. It's just you with seven or eight other guys and they have five or six counselors, teachers, and instructors there and you go through this entire re-introduction to Christianity, basically because we have this vision today in America of this almost feminized version of Jesus. It's Jesus with lipstick. He's pretty, his beard is all trimmed, he walks around in this glowing white robe.

The reality of it was, of course, a lot different. He was a carpenter and he certainly got his hands dirty. His disciples were fishermen and dockworkers. So the entire program is based on the Biblical concept of Isaiah 61.

When Jesus goes to the temple and confronts the Pharisees, they more or less say to him, "Who do you think you are?"

He pulls out the Torah and he turns to Isaiah 61 which reads:

The Spirit of the Lord God is upon me; because the Lord hath anointed me to preach good tidings unto the meek; he hath sent me to bind up the brokenhearted, to proclaim liberty to the captives, and the opening of the prison to them that are bound.

That's the whole purpose of ORW: to basically free these men who have had their hearts captured by warfare. To restore their warrior hearts. It's about the creation of fellowship between men who have experienced warfare in some form or other, the understanding of this primal need for fellowship, and an acceptance of how men love one another as brothers and warriors. Not something you learn at Sunday school.

I went on two of the ORW retreats. The first was out—way out—in the Virginia woods. The other was on the Eagle Ranch in Colorado. Yes. I needed to go a few times. Hard case.

I learned at ORW that I had been doing a few things right, even if by accident. I was talking to a lot of men who I suppose you could call my "mentors." There was a retired CIA officer named Peter B. who had worked counter intelligence for 30 years. And another CIA guy named Jim C. who had worked operations, but also ran afoul of the system at a few politically charged points in his career. A few years earlier during the Iraq war's darkest days, I had been mentored by General Wayne Downing and Colonel Mac Dorsey, who were both legendary Special Forces officers and knew their way around DC.

I had two mentors who also worked for me when I was in the Pentagon. My own personal Bagger Vances, after the Will Smith movie. I called them BV-1 and BV-2. Brian Berrey was BV-1, Bagger Vance 1. Coach, counselor, mentor and great friend. He was a former Navy SEAL and Blackwater operator. One of the smartest operational planners in the business. Kelly Snapp was BV-2, Bagger Vance 2. Coach, counselor, mentor and great friend. Kelly was one of the greatest communicators that I knew and had a way of boiling things down to what was important. The three of us were a formidable team in the Pentagon.

When I think about it, I had a number of mentors over the years, beginning with my father. You always have a lot to learn and the example and the wisdom of your elders is a good place to begin your education. Just sit and listen to the old guys and you are certain to learn a lot of things you would never get from just reading a book.

But I was doing a lot of that, too. And in the summer of 2011, I was invited to attend a program at the Claremont Institute where I became a Lincoln Fellow. This was a course—a sort of seminar or Platonic dialogue, even—that lasted six or seven intense days, in California, where I learned…well, how much I didn't know, up until then, about the American founding.

There was something else going on during these years. I was becoming more and more politically involved. This was inevitable, I suppose, since everything in Washington is political.

I had started out as a tech guy. But the longer I worked inside what many now call the Deep State, the more collisions I had with politics. And the more convinced I became that before we could get anything else right, we had to fix the politics. Otherwise ...

Well, things would go on as they had been since the day I sat on the small cement wall on West Side Highway with a member of the New York Fire Department and smoked cigarettes with guys working the rubble pile that, 48 hours earlier, had been the World Trade Towers. If things were going to change, then it had to start with the politics.

My "political awakening" —which may be too grand a way of putting it—came in multiple phases. The first was the frustration with what I saw going on, particularly in the Iraq War, which was so fundamentally mismanaged as to defy belief.

Obama's election really concerned me because I thought that he was overtly hostile toward what I felt America was. I mean, he didn't hide what he was from people who knew the ideological terrain. He described himself as a "community organizer," and that comes right out of Saul Alinsky's book *Rules for Radicals*. The complete phrase being "communist community organizer." But nobody seemed to question him about it and that just seemed strange. And dangerous.

And, then, we see the Obama administration in action. The overthrow of Gaddafi...the Arab Spring...the overtures to Iran. These things really woke me up. And when you looked around to find the resistance to all this, what you find is a cupcake, Mitt Romney, who even a month after Benghazi, just could not bring himself to hit Obama in the head with it.

Then, finally, Trump comes along…but that is getting ahead of the story.

In a way, my involvement in politics flowed out of the frustration that was set up by my work. Like I wrote earlier, I briefed people on the Hill. The Armed Service Committee, the Appropriations Committee, various intel committees. This generated relationships with Hill staffers and I was careful to maintain those relationships and I used the system to get things done. I didn't just sit in my cube living the inbox/outbox life. I was a change agent.

To be a change agent inside the system, you have to play the game. And you have to do it subtly. Which I did…for the most part. But I made some enemies and generated some resentments. Here I was, a mere GS-15; yet the Vice President's office knows who I am. The Senate Armed Services Committee Chairman knows who I am. A lot of people knew who I was because I'd been the guy pushing the counterterrorism envelope. The one who had revised the way we did targeting, had pushed the IED intelligence thing, had been very disruptive to the bureaucracy in what I thought was a healthy way. Because it *needed* to be disrupted.

So there would be scenes like the one where I was walking out of the Pentagon with my director who's a fairly senior guy approaching 70 years old and had been in the system forever. And General Mattis, who was at the time the United States Central Command (USCENTCOM) Commander came though the door and sayjng, "Hey, Rich, how's it going?"

That kind of thing will definitely polish up your creds…and stimulate resentment. But that is life inside the bureaucracy.

And if this stimulated resentments and I made enemies, it was never in a purely partisan fashion. I probably disliked the Republican Party *more* than the Democratic Party. I moved into the political world in support of the operational objectives that the department was trying to meet.

Then, when I was out of the government, that objective changed. Or shifted, anyway. Ever since the "red pill" briefing, I had been keeping up the effort to make people understand about Islam.

I would go up to the Hill, sometimes with Steve Coughlin, and we would brief people in Congress. Sometimes we would bring other people along. One time we had a third guy, a disruptor in his own right, from the National Counterterrorism Center. We had been asked by a junior staffer to come up and brief a new member who had come into office on the Tea Party Wave. His name was Jeff Duncan and he was from South Carolina. Played football at Clemson for a team that finished 7th in the national rankings in 1988.

His assistant—a woman named Rebecca—had blocked out four hours for our briefing because Duncan wanted to get up to steam on the War on Terrorism. We sat and briefed him on the evolutions of the war, the different things we thought he needed to know, the various players and actors operating here in the United States and abroad.

There was a point in the briefing where we talked about the Council of American-Islamic Relations (CAIR). We explained that this group had been created by Hamas—a group formally designated by the State Department as a Foreign Terrorist Organization (FTO)—to do media outreach in the United States, specifically, but also congressional outreach. It obviously couldn't do business as "Hamas" so it came up with CAIR.

But was all Hamas, all the same and all the time.

I asked the congressman, "Has CAIR been to see you yet?"

"No," he said.

"Well, they will be," I said.

He seemed a little puzzled and said, "Okay." Like it was a question.

"CAIR is operational," I said. "Here on Capitol Hill. It has people on staff up here, on several of the committees. It is a subversive organization. Spying and influence is what it does. Spying on members of Congress is part of the mission. An important part."

"Okay," he said. Again, sort of tentatively. His aide is there and she is reacting the same way. As though to say, "Where is all this going?"

"They'll be around," Coughlin said. "And when they come to see you, they will give you a form letter that says something like, 'if you have questions and concerns about Islam, then here is some contact information. And they will give you this book called *The Message of the Koran* and it will explain how Islam is a "religion of peace" and it will misquote and or omit verses from the actual Koran. The ones about deception and jihad."

By then, it was lunchtime and we had done pretty much what we came to do. The Congressman and his aide thanked us, but they seemed a little skeptical.

We saw ourselves out, left the Rayburn building, found ourselves a taxi and were heading off the Hill. We made it through one stoplight when the phone rang.

It was Rebecca, the congressman's aide.

"You won't believe who was just here," she said.

"CAIR, right?" I said.

"How did you know they were coming?"

"Because *they* knew <u>we</u> were coming. They probably have someone in your office. Or somebody in your office was talking to someone in another office about us and how we were coming up to brief your boss. Or, maybe, they are reading your e-mails. The important thing is ... they knew."

"But they walked in, literally, minutes after you left."

"Yep. That's what you're up against."

THE MEMO CONTINUED In candidate Trump, the opposition saw a threat to the "politically correct" enforcement narratives they've meticulously laid out over the past few decades.

In President Trump, they see a latent threat to continue that effort to ruinous effect and their retaliatory response reflects this fear.

12

MEETING DONALD
TRUMP

In addition to the networking and the briefing of people on the
Hill that had made it virtually inevitable that I would be drawn
into the political world, there was the Obama administration and its
policies, which were disastrous. Iran, Syria, Afghanistan, Libya, the
Arab Spring, China. It just went on and on. It was like we hadn't
learned anything from our past mistakes and were determined to just
go on making them over and over again. Mitt Romney's pitiful
campaign had failed and Obama was securely in the White House
and I just felt this sort of compulsion to *do something*. Through my
networking and the relationships I'd developed through my work on
Capitol Hill, I met people who lived and breathed politics.

I had briefed Louie Gohmert, the Tea Party congressman from
Texas and had gotten to know his Chief of Staff, Connie Hair. She

had been a writer for Human Events and is a force in conservative politics.

Connie introduced me to Sean Hannity. And that's how it went. You meet someone and you connect. You think the same way, politically, so you find yourself being introduced to other people who think like you. Pretty soon you are getting calls inviting you to meetings, asking you to have lunch or, in the case of Sean Hannity, to come on his radio show and, eventually, to guest host a few episodes.

So I had moved from doing secret work out of little offices and into the wide-open political spaces. I'd be lying if I said it wasn't heady stuff. I mean, who wouldn't be a little giddy over being introduced to Tucker Carlson or Sean Hannity. I was meeting the people behind the scenes as well. Learning what I could pick up here and there.

But that was the superficial side of it. Politics as show business. The feeling passes and you go back to work. And I wasn't ever really in awe of the media people in general. I'd been around people who did real things in the real world that inspired genuine awe. Like those truck drivers in Baghdad. And they weren't doing it for big bucks and the cheers of their adoring fans. They were doing it because...well, because they were American soldiers and the risks went with the job.

Still, I liked Sean Hannity and liked doing his radio show for him. It's fun to talk to people about the issues and get some back and forth going. Get their perspective on things and bounce things off of them. Especially if you can do it long form, which on the radio means ten or fifteen minutes. Not like TV where a minute or two is a long time.

I did some radio interviews and that led to calls asking me to do other shows. One connection led to another. Along the way, I was introduced to a movie producer named Ron Maxwell who lived in

Virginia, out of Washington, in the country. He had done the film version of the Jeff Shaara novel, *Gods and Generals,* and some other Civil War titles.

Well, we became friends and in November of 2015, I got a call from him. He wanted me to meet him at the Manassas Fairgrounds so he could introduce me to Donald Trump.

There was kind of a funny, maybe eerie coincidence at work here. Seven years earlier, I'd been living out near the Manassas Fairgrounds which is where, on the eve of the 2008 Presidential election, Obama had given his final campaign speech. It was his last stop because, well, Virginia was a 2008 battleground state and Manassas was the scene of the first big battle of the Civil War. That night, when I stood on the back porch of my house, I could hear Obama's voice, booming out from loudspeakers and echoing across the woods of Virginia. There was something ominous about the sound of that disconnected voice coming across the woods where all that blood had been shed. Hearing it, I felt something close to dread.

Now, here I was, in 2015, going back there to meet another candidate for President. One who was running against the entire Obama program and legacy.

I went with Steve Coughlin and we met up with Ron Maxwell at a coffee house in old town Manassas where we talked about Trump. He was still sort of a riddle to me but there were things I was hearing, and that he was saying, that I liked. About immigration and the border, for instance. And, of course, Iraq, Afghanistan...the whole "war on terror" fiasco.

But more importantly you can tell a lot about a candidate/politician by his opposition. Trump was opposed by all the right people: Wall Street, the Chamber of Commerce Republicans, Islamist apologists and the neocons. This was all one needed to know.

We drove up to the Fairgrounds, parked in the dirt field and made our way through security to a roped off section in the barn area for people who were going to have a chance to meet with Trump. This "grip and grin" scheduled to take place before he went out and gave his speech to a much bigger crowd in a much bigger barn.

The three of us, Ron, Steve, and I were introduced to Trump who gave us a wide, friendly smile. He looked at ease. Confident and focused on the task at hand. Trump reminded me of the men I had grown up around, no time for nonsense, fast talking, but still friendly and engaging in a way someone from New York, Philly or Boston would immediately recognize. This went against all the descriptions of him being hyper, almost manic.

We talked to him for a minute or two and brought up jihad and terrorism. This was around the time when Trump was catching a lot of flack for saying that there had been people in New Jersey and around the world that were celebrating on 9/11 after the buildings came down. We told him that we knew he had that right. He seemed to appreciate it.

He was relaxed in a way that doesn't come across when you see him on television. There was something almost—I don't know— *grandfatherly* about him. Successful. Confident. Cordial and polite. No stress. Maybe even enjoying himself. Not the hyper, angry person of the media images.

We didn't have a lot of time. There were about forty people there and everyone wanted a little time with Trump, so we only got two or three minutes. And then he had to move on because there was a caravan of black pastors that had come down from Philadelphia and they were going to announce their support for Trump. So he wanted to be sure to give them some time.

We went over to the main barn where he would be giving his speech and sat in this VIP area where Ron had tickets. There were maybe two thousand people in the crowd and there were no seats. But it didn't matter because people were excited and standing and you could just feel the energy coming off the crowd. It was absolutely electric. If I hadn't known it before then, it was very clear now that Trump had touched something in the psyche of a lot of Americans who were ... well, just fed up. With illegal immigration, pointless wars, and all the rest of it.

And Trump had a pitch-perfect, almost feral understanding of this. Right down to the music that was playing, when he mounted the stage to Twisted Sister playing "We're Not Going to Take It."

The crowd just exploded.

You couldn't be part of that scene without realizing that this was the real thing. There was a true connection between him and the people in that crowd and they just fed off each other's energy.

I would say I was an undecided skeptic about all of the Republican candidates before I went to that event. But I liked what I had been hearing about Trump's stance on immigration and on Islam. And I especially liked it that he didn't roll over for the media the way Mitt Romney had. That might have sealed the deal for me. Trump attacked the media. That's how he got his message out. He didn't allow the media to control him. He took it to them.

After meeting him, I was definitely a supporter.

I became active in the campaign. Not full time. I never quit my job but I did more appearances on Sean Hannity's show as someone with some experience in counterterrorism and Islam and was a Trump supporter.

The Islam issue was, of course, critical for me. If you watched what was going on in the world, you couldn't help but think that the jihadists were winning. When ISIS conquered Mosul in June of 2014, what else could you think. And there was the Arab Spring. We'd lost the initiative in Iraq and we were losing in Afghanistan after Obama had ordered a troop surge and then put a deadline on it. I mean, how clueless can you be? You call for a surge—with fewer troops than your own generals have said would be necessary for it to succeed. And then you announce a deadline for how long those troops are going to be there. This is the way we fight "violent extremism"? We tell the enemy what he needs to know in order to wait us out and then we tell our generals, "We will give you some troops. But not as many as you need."

We didn't tell Eisenhower he had to invade Europe with fewer divisions than he needed and that they had to be pulled out after six months. Wars don't work that way.

The generals knew it but they were, of course, complicit in their own way. They had been talking up progress in Afghanistan for as long as the war dragged on. It meant command. Promotions. People who are part of the Deep State are motivated by self-interest, just like everyone else. It was in their self-interest that we stay in Afghanistan. Until, of course, we could say "mission accomplished."

So the mission changed from finding and killing al Qaeda terrorists—to include Osama bin Laden—to nation building. To making it so Afghan girls could go to school and Afghan peasants could vote. Which, by the way, was a guarantee that Afghanistan would, like Iraq, have a Muslim dominated government.

I saw all this as just…well, *insane*. If our objective in Afghanistan was to create a liberal democracy based on the rule of law and all the rest of it, then we were going to be there for 100 years and we were going to have to kill a million people.

The war in Afghanistan is a pure example of the Deep State in action. Whole careers were built on that war. Massive contracts were let out. We constructed all kinds of things in that country. Twelve-thousand-foot runways, air-conditioned office complexes…twenty-first century infrastructure in a nation where many, many people still lived in mud huts.

The war generated countless conferences, studies, and fact-finding missions. We could have papered over the whole country with the reports that were written by all the experts. The war was studied and analyzed almost as much as it was fought. It was good for the Pentagon and the State Department and the whole Deep State foreign policy establishment, what some now call "the blob."

Not so good, though, for the American kids who got sent there to do an impossible job and got blown up and killed, or crippled for life or, even if they weren't physically injured, came home with PTSD.

We went in there to fight al Qaeda and kill Osama bin Laden. We broke up al Qaeda and we chased bin Laden into a hole. It took a while to find where he was roached up and kill him, but we finally did it.

And…still, four years after bin Laden's demise, we were stuck in Afghanistan and people were angry about that. And Trump was out there talking to them about it. He seemed to be the only one who, as they say, "got it." The only one who understood their anger, shared it and wanted to get us out of that war.

There was also Islam and the "religion of peace," doctrine which you disputed at risk to your career and good standing in the Deep State and the PC culture. It didn't seem to make any difference how many heads the jihadists were filmed sawing off, we were still supposed to buy into the "Islam is not even part of the problem" way of thinking.

Trump wasn't buying it and he gave voice to the feelings of a lot of people and helped them find their own.

I'd already been speaking out about this but now I had, on occasion, a platform where I could speak to large audiences. With the Hannity Show, in particular, the numbers were in the millions.

So, I took some opportunities to try to make the arguments in public that I had been making inside the Pentagon. That Islam was not "a religion of peace" and that we needed to understand that and deal with it.

During the summer of 2016, while Trump was campaigning, Sean Hannity invited me up to New York to host his afternoon radio show. It would be my first time in that role, so I was both excited and nervous. I knew I wasn't going to have a career in show business but still ...

Anyway, I got up to New York to do the show on July 5th and it turns out that is the day when there was big news from the director of the FBI, James Comey, a name we would become accustomed to hearing over the next months and years.

Comey held a press conference to announce the conclusions reached by the FBI in its investigation of Hillary Clinton's use of a private e-mail system and server, which she had destroyed. Along with at least 30,000 of her e-mails, some of which almost certainly contained classified information.

Comey, of course, made some tut tutting noises about this. Made it sound like Clinton was guilty of going seventy five in a sixty five zone and maybe even littering while she did it. Then Comey said there was not sufficient cause for criminal charges. Not even at the misdemeanor level. It was less than a slap on the wrist. It was a get-out-of-jail-free card. Even though there were people whose careers—military and otherwise—had been ruined for mishandling classified materials in a way that was far less serious and egregious. Those people went to jail, and Hillary Clinton went free.

Hillary, with the implicit blessings of James Comey, went on to run for President.

The Comey press conference was, needless to say, very big news. So big that Sean came back from vacation, into New York, so he could host the show that afternoon. He asked me to stay on as a guest on the show and then be the host the next day.

I stayed and one of the things I talked about on the show was Omar Mateen, who had killed forty-nine people in an Orlando nightclub, earlier in the summer. It was terrorism, pure and simple, but the usual evasions and equivocations were flying around. And when the FBI—*Comey's FBI*—released phone conversations between responders and the shooter, while he was still inside the nightclub, there were redactions. Which reminded me of nothing so much as the Pentagon and its way of dealing with Islamic terrorism. Deny its existence and suppress any evidence of it.

Still, it wasn't long before we learned what had been cut from the phone call transcripts. And it wasn't surprising.

The FBI had tried to excuse the initial redactions with one of those bureaucratically composed alibis. The Bureau's statement read:

"Unfortunately, the unreleased portions of the transcript that named the terrorist organizations and leaders have caused an unnecessary distraction from the hard work that the FBI and our law enforcement partners have been doing to investigate this heinous crime."

"As much of this information had been previously reported, we have re-issued the complete transcript to include these references in order to provide the highest level of transparency possible under the circumstances."

And what, exactly, had the FBI *not* wanted released to the public?

Just the shooter saying:

"Praise be to God, and prayers as well as peace be upon the prophet of God ... I pledge allegiance to Abu Bakr al-Baghdadi of the Islamic State."

It turned out, later, that both the shooter, and his father, were known to the FBI. In fact, the father had been an FBI informant. Probably the son too. Shortly after the shootings, the father appeared at a rally for Hillary Clinton and was seated on the same stage with her. Shockingly brazen.

Mateen's father claimed "Clinton is good for the United States versus Donald Trump." He said that he supported Hillary because she would also push for gun control, and she would be "good for national security."

Whose national security?

What he did not talk about was his satellite TV program targeting an audience of Pashtun Afghans who lived in America and Europe. The Taliban is heavily Pashtun. Mateen's show was strongly pro-Taliban and anti-American.

There was a lot of material for discussion there and I talked about it a lot when I did the Hannity shows, both as a guest and as the host. There was still a lot of denial out there and Hillary Clinton, among others, was feeding it. A lot of the people pushing that line were naive.

She was not.

I thought that was important. I thought, in short, that Hillary Clinton represented an existential threat to the United States as I knew it and loved it. That this was, as the famous essay put it, a "Flight 93 election."

So short of quitting my job and going to work full time for the campaign, I did all that I could to make sure that Donald Trump would be nominated and, then, elected.

Not long after I hosted Hannity's radio show, I was invited by my friend, Dave Brat's former Deputy Campaign Manager, Gray Delaney, to be a surrogate for Trump at the Republican National Convention in Cleveland. Gray was working on the surrogate placement team. The surrogate placement operation was run by the Bush and Romney crowd, which meant they had no understanding of Trump or his America First agenda. They thought that NeverTrumpers like John Bolton and Congressman Pete Sessions made good surrogates.

Gray's goal was to recruit surrogates who believed in "Make America Great Again" (MAGA) to counter the NeverTrumpers the RNC was placing. When Gray called, explaining Ken Cuccinelli was trying to block Trump's nomination by lining up hostile pro-Cruz delegations to block Trump's nomination, he said, "Please drop what you are doing and come to Cleveland—now!"

It didn't take much convincing; I knew what was at stake and I knew I needed to go.

Gray assigned me to the delegations his bosses told him to avoid, the ones so filled with the rabid Cruz supporters they seemed beyond reach. But I knew how to approach the Cruz supporters; many of my closest friends lived and died by Cruz's every word. I knew that if I focused on national security and immigration, they could be convinced to support Trump, even if reluctantly.

Congressman Louie Gohmert and I working radio row

The most problematic delegation was my home state of Virginia. Ken Cuccinelli, national director of Cruz's delegate operation, was the head of the delegation, and he aimed to deny Trump the nomination by ensuring there were more Cruz than Trump delegates at the convention.

Cuccinelli, the former Attorney General for the State of Virginia, had run for governor of Virginia in 2014 and, though he'd lost to Terry McAuliffe, he remained a big deal in the state's Republican Party machinery. More to the point, he was one of the fervent bitter enders trying to stave off Trump's nomination in Cleveland. And he knew how to play for the cameras. At one point, standing at a microphone arguing for a rules change, he abruptly threw his credentials on the floor and stormed dramatically away in a tantrum. It wasn't about principle. It was about power. His side had lost, fair and square, and he didn't like it. But it was effective television.

And though Trump had won a majority of the primaries, Cruz had a better grassroots operation. Even at this late date there was a chance Cuccinelli's Hail Mary operation might succeed

Working with the staffer assigned to select speakers for the Virginia delegation, Gray arranged to have former University of Virginia Professor David Jordan—once President Reagan's ambassador to Peru—and me speak for a total of 45 minutes on the morning of Monday, July 18th.

But when Cuccinelli caught wind of it, Gray got a Sunday night call letting him know the Ambassador and I would be restricted to a mere ten minutes, and strongly suggesting it wasn't worth the bother.

No way I was coming all this way to *not* address my home state.

Unbelievably, when I arrived at the breakfast meeting, Cuccinelli tried to keep me from doing my briefing. I didn't throw a tantrum in response, or toss my notes on the floor. Just waited around until the cavalry arrived.

Meanwhile, Cuccinelli's security people were actually physically preventing Ambassador David Jordan from entering the facility. Scholarly and reserved, he is a man of endless civility and patience, but both were now sorely tried by the Virginia delegation's obstructionism. "Do you know who I am?" he demanded. "I am a United States Ambassador and I was nearly killed twice during my service in Lima. I am not letting you keep us from giving this briefing."

He was having *none* of what Cuccinelli and his crowd were trying to pull off!

Ambassador Jordan dressing down RPV Executive Director John Findlay

Former Republican National Committee (RNC) Chair Ed Gillespie was also on hand, and he likewise fell squarely into the establishment Trump opposition camp. Ironically enough, his security that day was provided by an old friend of mine, Frank, a former DC cop. We just smiled at one another as we watched the politicals jockeying around us.

Then the cavalry arrived.

Supreme Court Justice Clarence Thomas' wife, Ginni, is a force in the Republican Party in Virginia, and someone I had come to know as a fellow staunch conservative. She appeared moments after I'd been informed by Cuccinelli's staffers that my briefing to the delegation was off. Spotting me, she asked what was going on and I told her. She walked me past the staffers and directly to Cucinelli saying, "Ken, do you know my friend Rich? He's speaking to us today."

Cucinelli got this look on his face like somebody had dumped his Cheerios all over his lap. I gave the briefing.

Two footnotes to this story: Gray Delany, who'd recruited me, was soon fired for the outrage of trying to place pro-Trump surrogates in hostile delegations, and otherwise help Trump at his own convention.

It was collateral damage, and most unfortunate. But as far as the NeverTrumpers were concerned, the damage was done. By then, I had personally already briefed three delegations, as had my colleagues – all of us considered by the RNC so extreme we should probably have been sent instead to Guantanamo. The operation was a success. Several of the states we briefed ended up voting for Trump on the first ballot, as Cruz and his dead enders were humiliated on the national stage.

Ginni Thomas had been a Ted Cruz supporter, like Cucinelli, but when she realized how things were going, she became a Trump backer. And, after a while, Cucinelli did too. In fact, he went to work for the Trump administration. In late 2019, he was Principal Deputy Director of the U.S. Citizenship and Immigration Services (USCIS) agency and then became Acting Deputy Secretary of Homeland Security for the Trump Administration.

This episode wasn't important in the great scheme of things. Just a little hissy fit by someone who was upset because things hadn't gone his way. But...already at the Cleveland convention, with Trump having the nomination sewed up, there was this tension between the people who had been with him from the beginning and the people who had opposed him and then climbed aboard the bandwagon for the ride—and the job in Washington—once he'd won.

The original Trump supporters—the people who had been with him through the campaign, going back to the days when nobody thought he had a chance and had stayed with him though all the crazy swings and through every crisis when he looked like he didn't have a chance and might have to withdraw…those people were not traditional Republicans. In fact, a lot of them were not Republicans at all. A lot of them were like me. They hated the Republican establishment and saw it as the enemy.

That's because the Republican establishment is basically the party of the Chamber of Commerce and what Eisenhower called the "Military Industrial Complex." That's who the people running for office and getting elected listen to and serve. If the Chamber wants cheap labor, they get it, and the institutional Republicans don't care and they also lie about it. The same thing is true of the wars that we can't win and we can't get out of. The people who voted for Trump in the primaries were voting against the Chamber of Commerce as well as the perpetual war machine.

The traditional Republicans at first didn't understand what was happening to them and, when they did finally begin to understand, they wouldn't—actually, *couldn't*—accept it, even though it had been happening for several election cycles. You have a Tea Party election in 2010 and the people who made it happen, the *voters,* get screwed by the people they elected. Obamacare is not repealed. Spending does not go down. Immigration—especially illegal immigration—remains out of control…probably because the Chamber Republicans want it that way. Cheap labor, you know.

And the Republicans who are running things in the House of Representatives are fine with that. They are in Washington, living the life, and the voters who put them there...well, they are even more angry then they had been. And the signs were there, for anyone with the eyes to see. In 2014, those angry people went to the polls in Virginia and voted in a primary against one of the Republicans' biggest stars. (And, incidentally, biggest frauds.)

Eric Cantor was the quintessential Republican In Name Only (RINO). He represented a district that included Richmond and he was a career politician right down to his toes. He may have once thought he was getting into politics to do good when, in fact, what happened is...he did well.

He and his wife made lots of money. They lived the prosperous, Washington insider life. They were quite the power couple, Cantor's wife worked on Wall Street and made a pile of money leveraging her access to the Majority Leader. And, predictably, Cantor's votes were somehow always Wall Street friendly. He only voted to do something about the debt when his party was in the minority and the measure was sure to lose. That way, he could go back to his constituents and tell them that he was a good fiscal conservative when he was, in truth, a big-government corporate Republican.

And, typical of the breed, he didn't appreciate—didn't even know—that his constituents had caught on to his act. He dismissed them as ignorant peasants, deplorables that he could convince he was one of them with a couple slick mailers. His constituents didn't buy it, and he lost a primary election to a complete unknown at the time, Dave Brat. All the wise men and women of the Deep State and the media were shocked. It came as a complete surprise to them, but not to the people they held in disdain while they expected to get their votes, almost as though they were an entitlement.

But still, after the Tea Party election and Cantor's shocking loss, the old guard Republicans just didn't get it. Or wouldn't accept it.

They had started out thinking that for 2016, their guy would be Jeb Bush who was so disconnected, so clueless about the anger of people whose votes he expected to get, almost like they were an entitlement, that he would say he believed, "Immigration is an act of love." Through the old money networks, he raised $80 million or so and promptly blew it in the primaries, none of which he won or even came close to winning.

Jeb, like his supporters and backers, didn't get it. Neither did the other candidates and their supporters.

Trump got it.

He understood the kind of Americans that Bush ignored and Hillary Clinton would famously call "deplorables." He understood they cared about immigration and they weren't sentimental about it. To them it was an issue about crime, salary, and what kind of country they were living in and that their children were growing up in. It was about sovereignty, culture, language. Our original motto—E. Pluribus Unum—means "From many, one." Not "from many, many." It's the complete opposite of multiculturalism.

The "deplorables" cared about Islam—specifically Islamic supremacy. And they didn't buy into the "religion of peace," line. If Islam was about peace then why were so many of their sons and daughters going to war in Islamic countries. Because it was *their* sons and daughters who were doing the fighting. Not the children of the elites, Republican and Democrat, who were going to expensive schools and landing jobs on Wall Street.

They cared about the things that just didn't seem to concern the country club, boardroom Republicans. They cared about debt finance. They cared about the opioid crisis. They cared about the rule of law. They actually gave a damn. And the establishment guys, the opportunist guys party types around the campaign never understood that. They underestimated the number of Americans whose sense of grievance and anger was given voice by Trump.

Trump got it. He understood how frustrated and angry these people were. How they felt when they elected Republicans in a landslide Tea Party election and, before that, elected George W. Bush and then re-elected him when he was so clearly not a loved figure, like Ronald Reagan, and *still* the country never moved to the right. So in their desperation and in their frustration, they were backing Donald Trump. They were willing to forgive his impolitic bullshit in order to get a guy who was willing to fight.

That was the key.

Trump fights.

He may not win the war, or even every battle, but he was not going to allow America to "change" quietly. "Managed decline" or whatever the globalists, socialists, and corporatists had called it was not going to happen on his watch.

Trump was the counterrevolutionary candidate.

In my thinking, there were two or three skills that really made the difference. That made Trump…Trump.

First, because he had experience in reality TV, he knew that all politics is theater. You saw it at the convention in Cleveland. He sensed that when Ted Cruz went up to the podium to speak, he was not going to be delivering any endorsement.

So, sure enough, Cruz wraps up his speech without an endorsement of Tump and the crowd starts booing. And at that moment, into the convention hall walks Donald Trump. With his beautiful family. And the crowd goes wild. He won the moment. The night. The convention. Because he knew how to work the cameras like that.

A second important, even crucial, quality about Trump is that he does not buy into the PC way people see the world. He refuses to abide by it because he recognizes that "political correctness" — AKA cultural Marxism—is an enforcement and control mechanism. Trump refused to be controlled. Political Correctness is always about power, not virtue. And people get that and they resent it and they want to push back. Like Trump.

There is also this third thing about Trump...he is a master at generating his own image, his Trump brand if you will. Some people don't like this trait, and claim that he is a narcissist, and they see him as kind of evil. But in reality, his ability to create that Trump brand, and fight to maintain that image is a shield against the relentless attacks directed at him. And Trump's ability to do that is so strong that, in some cases, he could hold on to his own sense of self and self-image in spite of his political opponents' 24-7 attacks against him.

This quality of his allowed him to withstand the utter onslaught that came against him. An onslaught that most politicians, even really strong ones, would not have been able to withstand. But, somehow, he was not only able to withstand these attacks, he was actually *strengthened* by them. Because he was not just unwilling, he was *incapable* of internalizing their slanders or their smears. Trump supporters saw those attacks by political, media, and academic establishment figures not as attacks against candidate Trump, but as attacks against his supporters, further fueling their anger.

The Bible is full of flawed people that God uses to do amazing things. I see that in Trump. And I guess it might explain, in a way, why even most of the people around him never understood his success.

As a matter of fact, I think you can make a pretty compelling argument that the Republican Party establishment was Trump's and remains Trump's greatest threat. It's the Republican Party that didn't do the Obamacare thing he wanted. It's the Republican Party that would not adjourn Congress the first two years of the Trump presidency to allow him to make recess appointments. It's the Republican Party that fought him on a lot of his policy objectives on immigration, on the Islam issue, and on and on. Guys like Paul Ryan and Mitt Romney are a far greater threat to Trump's MAGA agenda than Nancy Pelosi or Chuck Schumer.

But that came later. First, Trump had to get elected. And I did my bit to help.

THE MEMO CONTINUED Through the campaign, candidate Trump tapped into a deep vein of concern among many citizens that America is at risk and is slipping away.

13

A NIGHT FOR THE AGES

After Cleveland, I did what I could for the campaign whenever I had the time and an opportunity. I continued giving briefings in my role as a surrogate. I met with some groups in Virginia. I made myself available when people were looking for advice on issues where I had some expertise. Particularly, of course, counterterrorism. I was asked by Senator Jeff Sessions to serve the campaign as a counterterrorism advisor. And that was a big thing since that was my turf. I knew the issues and I had been briefing on them for a long time now and doing it for some tough audiences, especially in the Pentagon. I'd done a year on the faculty of National Defense University and that helped me master the skills you need to hold the attention of an audience. In August, there was a meeting in New York, in Trump Tower, with the candidate and several people from the campaign and Sessions, again, invited me to attend. To the extent that you could even call it an "invitation," it wasn't the sort of thing you are likely to turn down.

Before the meeting, I was introduced to some of Trump's family. I met Ivanka and she was very pretty, friendly and welcoming.

There were two or three dozen of us and we were there to talk about national security. General Mike Flynn was there. Sessions. Rudy Giuliani. Several people from the House of Representatives to include Peter King, Chris Collins, and Lou Barletta. Among others.

Once the meeting started it was clear that Trump had a good understanding of the terrorism threat and the ideological drivers behind it. I was pretty junior in that crowd so I just sat there and listened for the first part of the meeting. Then, we got to the Islamic State of Iraq and Syria (ISIS). He had been saying in the campaign that Obama wasn't doing enough about ISIS and when he got to the White House, this would change. He wanted ISIS defeated and gone.

"Maybe I ought to say that we should declare war on ISIS," he said.

There wasn't any real pushback in the room. Not much in the way of support for that, either. The idea just sort of sat out there.

I thought declaring war was a *terrible* idea. Was sure of it, in fact. One of the big concerns in the campaign was women voters. Trump had enough problems there without talking about how he was going to declare war. That was a sure way to lose women's votes.

I raised my hand.

"Sir."

It was like the scene from *The Hunt For Red October* where Jack Ryan, the junior analyst who is a nobody to everyone in a room full of admirals and generals and cabinet officers, presumes to advise the President of the United States. Well, maybe not *that* intense but it was one of those moments when you feel the way you do when you are standing at the window of a very tall building and looking down. Way down. Or maybe when you are standing in an airplane door, about to make your first parachute jump.

It was too late to turn back so I said my piece.

"Sir," I said, "you don't need to do that."

Everyone in the room looked at me.

"It's very close in states you're going to need and you don't need to scare off *any* voters. And you don't need a declaration of war to do whatever you need to do to defeat ISIS. You already have all the authority you need. And you really don't want to empower Congress by asking them for a declaration of war when it comes to dealing with ISIS."

While I was explaining about Congress, Sessions leaned over to Trump and said, "He's right, Sir."

So, that was my moment and my contribution. And who knows? I may have saved him some votes in some battleground state.

One other thing about that meeting…a late addition to the list of invitees was Steve Bannon, who would become CEO of the campaign. This was going to be announced in a couple of days.

Bannon was being talked up as the "big idea" guy who was going to energize the campaign. It was part of a reshuffling. Manafort would be gone. Bannon and Kellyanne Conway would be in.

Bannon didn't have a lot to do with the national security side of the campaign. That wasn't his focus at the time, so he didn't have a lot to say at this meeting. He was the political guy with the big ideas and he got it about Trump. He understood that this was a true change election and that Trump was not the candidate of the old Republican party. This was something that people at that meeting – and a lot of others like it – didn't get. Still don't.

But what Bannon didn't get, until it was too late, was that if this was going to be a change election, and our team won, then it was going to have to result in a change administration. And that came down to the people who would be staffing it. This may have seemed like a sort of theoretical question at the time. There was a little more than two months left before the election and Trump was behind in the polls and people in the press were talking—*assuming*, actually— that it would result in a landslide win for Clinton.

So maybe it was a little premature to be thinking about who was going to be serving in the administration. As, say, Secretary of Defense or National Security Advisor or...whatever.

But we learned, to our dismay, that this was probably *exactly* the time for Bannon—and Trump—to be thinking about that. Because, as it turned out, when they did win, they were unprepared for what came next. And that led to some very bad outcomes, the effects of which the administration and the country are still feeling.

But that is for later. For now...back to that meeting in the Trump Tower.

When it was over, I got the train back to Washington and I kept doing what I had been doing. But I also had email exchanges and a few short conversations with Bannon, Sessions, and Mike Flynn about the campaign's positions on this or that issue as it related to national security. And, like a lot of people, I followed the campaign through the media and I felt, somehow, like they might just be getting it wrong. That maybe it wasn't going to be the walkover for Hillary Clinton that she, her campaign, and her enablers in the media all thought it was going to be.

I can't say I ever thought it was in the bag, that I was sure Trump would win, but I felt like there was something that the media was missing and that it would turn out to be important.

That missing thing was...well, guys like me. Like my family anyways. Working class guys. White, Black, Hispanic. The guys who fix your plumbing when it's broken. The guys who work in a factory. The guys who have to work two jobs, work one-hundred-hour weeks just to stay even, who are always treading water and feel like they are about to drown.

These guys didn't even bother to vote in the 2012 election because...you know, what difference does it make. They're all the same.

Trump was speaking to those guys and while I'm not, technically, still one of them because I work in Washington and I'm doing okay, the roots are so deep that I still get it.

And while I'm reading all the stories in the mainstream media about how Hillary is going to win this thing going away and isn't it wonderful how she is going to shatter the glass ceiling...all this time, I'm thinking that there are a lot of guys like me out there and while we may not have even voted in past elections, we will be turning out big for this one.

But, then, maybe this was all just wishful thinking.

Then again...maybe not.

We'd find out soon enough.

So...on election day 2016, I took the Amtrak from Washington to New York where I would be watching the returns, with other Trump supporters, in a ballroom at the Hilton, and when Karen and Billy Vaughn insisted I ride up to New York with them, I agreed. After all, if Trump won, then it would be the memory of a lifetime.

In any case, it would have been hard for me to turn Karen and Billy down. We'd become friends after their son, Aaron, was killed in Afghanistan along with several other members of SEAL Team 6, in Wardak Province—horribly—in August of 2011. They were serving as an Immediate Response Force (IRF) supporting the Rangers and when their chopper, a Chinook with the call sign *Extortion 17*, approached the Landing Zone (LZ), the Taliban fired three rocket propelled grenades (RPGs). Two missed but a freak, "one-in-a-million" shot caught one of the rotors and sheered ten feet off the blade. The chopper went down hard, blew up and burned. All aboard were killed.

It was the kind of thing that raises the sort of questions that inevitably followed. Why that chopper, an old Chinook, when a more advanced, better performing model existed? Why hadn't there been airstrikes to prep the LZ? And why, for that matter, were the SEALs involved in the first place?

Things happen in war. Especially that war. Still, Karen and Billy had a lot of questions, not the least of which was why a Muslim Imam had prayed over the bodies of the dead, which included seven Afghan soldiers who'd been along on the mission. According to one account: *As US war heroes lay in their caskets before their last flight home, the Imam damned America's fallen warriors as "infidels" who would burn in hell. As US military leaders observed the ceremony at Bagram Air Base, the Imam boasted over the deaths of US heroes with words such as, "The companions of heaven [Muslims] are the winners."*

In time, I became very close to the Vaughns. The three of us were Christians, something that helped them get through the pain of losing their son. And, we were all supporters of Trump and fierce in our opposition to Obama. Karen had written a letter for public circulation demanding that he resign. Like a lot of other Americans, the three of us were sick of that war in Afghanistan which was fifteen years old, and counting, and still costing the lives of American men, like their son. Karen had made a very moving speech at the Republican National Convention that nominated Trump and a little later on she came to the rescue after a man named Khizr Khan—a gold star parent whose Muslim son had been killed in Afghanistan—had given a tough speech at the Democratic convention that led to calls for Trump to leave the race. Karen organized an event in Florida where Trump met with her and with other Gold Star families and that calmed those waters.

But even before that and before the convention, Karen was well known by people in the campaign. She was a force.

"Don't worry," she said, on election day. "Come with us. It'll be fun. I'll get the two of you in." The other one of the two of us being my then-girlfriend and now wife, also "Karin."

Karen (Vaughn) was not someone you could easily say "no" to and she was probably right that, win or lose, it would be "fun." And if it did turn out to be a **W,** then it would be a lot more than just fun. It would be something to remember for the rest of my life: a night when history was made.

The ballroom at the Hilton was not large, as those things go, which might have been a sort of statement. It was early evening when we got there and the room was still filling up. A lot of the Trump supporters were putting on a game face, but almost everyone in the country felt Trump would lose. If they were correct, and things did not go our way, Trump might come by himself later in the evening to give a concession speech and maybe there was some consolation in that.

Still...there was a certain kind of buzz in the room. A little crackling of electricity in the air. Trump supporters were used to hearing that their man had no chance. We'd been hearing it ever since he announced, and throughout the primaries, that he wasn't supposed to win right up to the convention where he wasn't supposed to get the nomination. And, then, through all the various crises and calls for him to get out after he was the nominee.

And now, on election day, he—and we – were still here.

I believed that there were a lot of people, like me, who thought he was going to win even before the first surprising returns began to come in. There were too many people who'd had enough. Too many people like me.

Ordinarily, I might have felt out of place at a political event like this but, that night, I was feeling something much stronger than social unease or strangeness. It was a sense that something totally unexpected by all "experts" was about the happen and blindside them and at least half the country.

If, as I believed, the "experts" were wrong, it surely wouldn't be the first time. In fifteen years of working counterterrorism, in and out of the government, I had seen it over and over. Because we were listening to those "experts," we were still making the same mistakes we had been making when the World Trade Center towers came down and the "war on terror" began. Mistakes that we would go on making if Hillary Clinton won the election. As, of course, all the smart people said she would.

At first, the mood in the room was, I suppose, a kind of forced cheerfulness. People were chatting and sipping their drinks and there was music. I knew some of the people in the room. I'd had conversations with Erik Prince and with Jeff Sessions and other people connected with the Trump campaign. We would exchange a few words and keep the game face on. Nobody was saying it was a solid lock or anything like that. But there were people who, like me, believed things would go Trump's way. Believed it even after the first exit polling data was broadcast, shortly after five, showing that Hillary Clinton would be elected President of the United States and the people who were looking into the camera and reading the news couldn't conceal their satisfaction.

The good news, I thought, was that they had been wrong so many times before.

There was background music. A bar where I got something to drink. A stage adorned with flags. Big screens on the wall where the numbers, as they came in, would be played. All those months of campaigning, fund raising, "expert analysis," scandals like the Billy Bush tape...that was all behind us in the rear-view mirror. Now it was time to wait.

Nervously.

The actual returns starting coming in almost as soon as the polls closed, and Trump was losing, at first, but not as badly as the predictions would have had it. Then, things in Florida started to go against the way the "elite" had all said they would. You didn't have to know much about voting patterns in that state to know that the counties in the Panhandle were on Central Time, so the polls there closed an hour after they did in the rest of the state. If it was close in Dade and Broward counties, then the returns from the Panhandle could tip things our way.

It was closer than expected in those counties and also in some places in the state where a lot of the people were retirees from the mid-West. From places like Chicago, Detroit, and Cleveland. Places with a lot of blue-collar voters like my father. And me.

These parts of Florida started coming in showing Trump. Two or three hours into the networks' election night broadcasts, people around the country were starting to get the sense that something was happening. Something unexpected.

I had a red *Make America Great Again* hat on my head and a drink in my hand and, like a lot of the people in that room, I was starting to get the feeling. It had been a long time of feeling somehow, marginalized. Of being led by people who claimed to know better than we. Many of whom thought they *were better* than we. Who considered us "deplorables."

It was looking like we might finally have our night.

The returns from North Carolina, Pennsylvania, Ohio, even *Wisconsin* were looking good and the weight of a lot of frustrating times and experiences seemed to be lifting. I'd been to the rubble pile that had been the World Trade Center towers. I'd been to Baghdad a few weeks after the statue of Saddam Hussein had come down, when the city was experiencing a siege of bombings and people like me were trying to devise tactics for dealing with the weapons we called IEDs. I had fought the bureaucratic wars in the Pentagon. Been the subject of an IG investigation and been exonerated. I had been educated and self-educated on the nature, history, theology, and jurisprudence of Islam and had been exiled from the Pentagon for my troubles. I had spent my exile at the National Defense University where I studied Islam and then stayed on as faculty. I had briefed senior people in the Pentagon and Congress—people like Admiral Erik Olson and Senator Jim Talent—on the weapons we were facing in Iraq and Afghanistan. I had felt, many times, like it just might be hopeless. That there were too many powerful people with too much invested in the status quo for things to fundamentally change. That if change did come, it would almost certainly be too late and too little. That there were too many people with power who, if they did not want the United States of America to lose, certainly wanted it to change into something that my father and people like him would not recognize.

Even if people didn't realize it, the Trump campaign had been a crusade against all of this. Against soft surrender to China's game of economic hardball and acquiescence to its military buildup and expansion. Against making more wars in the mid-East—like in Libya—when we were bogged down in fights we had started years ago and couldn't finish. Against opening the borders to anyone who wanted to cross them for whatever reasons and in whatever numbers. Against...*all of this*. It was a crusade, like it said on my hat, to Make America Great Again.

The night went on, but it didn't drag. Instead, the pace seemed to pick up. We got North Carolina. Michigan was up in the air and that was a good sign. People were now thinking, "Hey, we can *do this.*"

Then it was, "Okay, good, we're neck and neck in Pennsylvania. We got Ohio ..."

And people could see that the blue wall was crumbling and the air in that room was just electric.

And finally at one-thirty in the morning, they call Pennsylvania and the news we have been waiting for goes out on those big television screens that are all around the room. The blue wall is breached.

Then. Nothing. For an hour. Nobody in the national media was willing to call the race. Like a prize-fight which had gone 12 rounds and awaited the judges' decision. The media simply could not bring itself to accept *reality*. The narrative machine had hit a glitch.

Finally, at 2:29AM on Nov 9, the Associated Press reported Donald Trump has been elected President of the United States. And the crowd on the floor just exploded.

There were police officers literally with tears, literally, in their eyes. I saw an old woman on her knees praying. I saw some short-haired guys—military or cops or something but dressed in suits—turn to the media and just start screaming at them, "Fuck you. You bunch of liars. Fake News!!!" Just screaming, "You people need to be ashamed of yourselves."

It was just an amazing experience to be part of it all. To be there and holding my little "Veterans for Trump" sign. It was just so great. The sort of experience where you wish the feeling would never end.

Finally, at almost three o'clock in the morning, Trump took the stage to make his victory speech. He looked buoyant and content. His wife, Melania, looked radiant. He said a few words and the room ate them up. He had done it. *We* had done it.

Robert Matheson, Ron Maxwell and I at Trump's New York victory party

We finally went to sleep at about 5:00 in the morning. Got up later and walked from the Hyatt midtown to Penn Station to get the Amtrak back to Washington. I carried my little "Veterans for Trump" sign and every single cop that we saw between the Hyatt Midtown and Penn Station—every single one —gave me the thumbs up, head nod, congrats, or "just wanna say, 'thank you.'"

Maybe twenty-five cops signaled me. And then, there were people who gave me a look that was just filled with scorn and hatred, imagining that you're a white supremacist, racist, Nazi. And then you had guys just cheering you. And a lot of people giving you a thumbs up just, like, quietly.

Because it's New York.

And, then, back to Washington where I expected I would soon be going to work in the White House.

It would be my second tour of duty there.

THE MEMO CONTINUED Because candidate Trump publicly exposed the Republican Establishment for their duplicitous activities, they are at risk as long as Trump can turn on them and are, therefore, bitter foes. Candidate Trump's success remains an ongoing existential threat to establishment Republicans.

14

INSIDE THE WIRE: A
FIGHT TRANSFORMED

The floor of the Hilton ballroom had not been swept up before you began hearing the words "resistance" and "impeachment." It came from places that were expected but also some that were surprising…and alarming.

There was actually speculation about impeachment even *before* Trump had become the Republican nominee. In April of 2016, *Politico* published a piece reporting that,

> "Impeachment" is already on the lips of pundits, newspaper editorials, constitutional scholars, and even a few members of Congress. From the right, Washington attorney Bruce Fein puts the odds at 50/50 that a President Trump commits impeachable offenses as president. Liberal Florida Rep. Alan Grayson says Trump's insistence on building a wall at the U.S.-Mexico border, if concrete was poured despite Congress's

opposition, could lead down a path toward impeachment.
Even the mainstream Republican head of the U.S. Chamber
of Commerce recently tossed out the I-word when discussing
the civilian backlash if Trump's trade war with China led to
higher prices on everyday items sold at WalMart and Target.
On his radio show last month, Rush Limbaugh even put a
very brisk timeline on it: "They'll be talking impeachment on
day two, after the first Trump executive order," he said.

And it wasn't long after Trump had taken the oath, for the talk
to get serious and even move beyond mere impeachment.

For instance, Rosa Brooks, a law professor from Georgetown
University who had been a senior Pentagon advisor during the
Obama years wrote that "Trump's first week as president has made it
all too clear" [that] "he is as crazy as everyone feared" [and that one]
"possibility is one that until recently I would have said was unthinkable in the United States of America: a military coup, or at least a
refusal by military leaders to obey certain orders."

This was coming from a member in good standing of the Deep
State. And there was a lot more like it, coming both from inside the
administration and outside of it. It came from people who worked in
plain view and it came, as we have learned, from people who worked
in the shadows and in the dark corners of the Deep State. It came
from Democrats, of course. And it came, surprisingly (to some),
from Republicans.

And their efforts might have been among the most effective.

Much of what government does is a function of personnel.
People make policy, of course. But people also implement those
policies.

Or not, in the event they are opposed to those policies and can get away with derailing them.

The voters can elect a candidate who promises to, say, end the country's military presence in Afghanistan because fifteen years of fighting in that godforsaken, Third World dump seems like enough. But that doesn't necessarily mean it is going to happen. Even when the person who was elected meant what he said and wants to make it happen.

That person may encounter resistance to leaving Afghanistan from within his own government. From people who are part of the permanent Washington/government/media/legal/lobbying establishment. They have their own agenda and they may not be inclined to abandon it just because an election didn't go their way. They have built careers and reputations on that war and they aren't ready to quit just because it is clearly un-winnable. As long as the troops stay, those people can keep making policy and rising in the ranks of the bureaucracy. Military and civilian.

I'd been inside the government and I'd seen it. I knew how it worked. I had, in fact, been something of an insurgent myself. I'd fought against policies that came down from the top. First, when I was trying to get us to focus on IEDs and counterinsurgency in Iraq. And then when I was trying to move our understanding of the role of Islam in what we were calling the "war on terror." But I never tried to sabotage polices I was opposed to or plans that I thought wouldn't work. I tried to reform those policies and change those plans and I did my job as well as I could do it. And I'd never gone after someone and tried to get him railroaded out of the government and sent to prison. Which is how the Deep State does things.

I'd taken my share of hits. To include that IG investigation that came up with nothing except proof of bending some administrative rules. And, then—mostly because of my stance on Islam—I became radioactive enough that my boss at the CTTSO sent me away to the National Defense University.

I had gone back to the Pentagon but there weren't any parades upon my return. I saw the shape of the shadows on the wall and I left government, but I didn't leave the world of counterterrorism. And, as I have written earlier, I began to get active in politics.

Change, I realized, was not going to come from within. Not while Obama —a disciple of Saul Alinsky—was President and certainly not if Hillary Clinton, another Alinskyite, followed him. The hole we had been digging ourselves into would just get deeper.

Too deep, perhaps, to crawl out of.

I had done my bit for the Trump campaign. Which, to be honest, I didn't think of as a Republican enterprise. This was not Mitt Romney *redux*. Trump was not just "unconventional" and not simply "extreme." He was something different.

I believe Trump won the election in the first debate when Megan Kelly asked him, "Will you back the Republican candidate?"

And Trump's answer, basically was, if not "no," then "it depends."

At that point, he basically became a third-party candidate. Then he hijacked the Republican ticket and bent it to his purposes. But he was never a traditional, conventional Republican and that, of course, is *why* he was elected. He was taking on all the forces that had been in charge and running things that millions of Americans were not just frustrated with, and opposed to, but actually hated.

They hated being screwed over and they hated being called "deplorables," by people who considered themselves "elites." They hated the way they were depicted in the media and by Hollywood. They hated the way our manufacturing jobs had gone to China and other nations where the labor was cheap and the air and the water were dirty. They hated what was happening to the country under the rule of the Uniparty and they wanted...well, they wanted to do what Trump said he was going to do.

They wanted to "Make America Great Again."

So that was the mandate. And when Trump tried to act on it, he ran into resistance. Right from the start. Even before he was sworn into office. It began, in fact, before he had even been elected. There had actually been pressure on him, from the Republican establishment, to resign the nomination, if "resign" is the right word. The scenario was that he would hand the nomination over to Pence who was a conventional Republican pol and not, like Trump, a disruptor. The pressure was especially intense after a tape came out with Trump talking about women and how he would "grab 'em by the pussy."

The other person on the tape was Billy Bush. So a member of the Bush family, which was the soul of the anti-Trump wing of the Republican establishment, had a tape that looked, for 48 hours or so, like it might bring down the Trump nomination and hand it over to Mike Pence and the old guard. There was even speculation, during the panic over that tape, about who would be named to take the place of Pence on the ticket. One name you heard a lot was that of Condoleezza Rice, former Bush Secretary of State. The one with those otherworldly ideas about a democratic Iraq that she somehow believed had moved beyond tribalism and 5,000 years of history.

If you were a loyal Trump supporter, it wasn't hard to imagine that you were up against something that went beyond the normal. There were people, and I knew some of them, who believed that we were dealing with conspiracies.

Turns out, of course, that they were right. "Crossfire Hurricane" was a conspiracy of people within the government. Within the FBI and other elements of the Intelligence Community. It was a secret, illegal operation the objective of which was…take down Trump.

But there was conspiracy to damage Trump and his presidency at a more prosaic level. One that wasn't illegal so much as it was selfish and immoral. The objective of this conspiracy was to ensure that a Trump Administration was not staffed with the MAGA people who had worked to get him the nomination and then win the election, but with old time Republican party hacks in general and, in the national security sphere especially…with neocons. The same people who had fought against him when he was campaigning for the nomination and, in some cases, after he'd won it. The kind of people, in other words, who had gotten us into Iraq and Afghanistan and these endless, and now pointless, wars. And who didn't want us to get out of them. Who were committed to wars that might not be endless but that certainly had no end in sight.

Even before the election, Trump had made Chris Christie the guy in charge of staffing. If, and when, Trump won the election, Christie would be selecting the people he needed for his team and they would be ready to hit the ground running.

Well…pretty to think so.

But in the first place, Christie was a RINO and not a MAGA guy at all. He had been one of Trump's opponents in the early primaries and when it was clear he wasn't going anywhere, he'd dropped out and endorsed Trump. The better to land a cabinet job, maybe, or even be picked as Trump's running mate, if he got the nomination.

Well, that didn't happen. I think that's because Trump realized that, even in the world of politics, Christie didn't test real high on loyalty. It's like the old line about how he was a "good and faithful servant…off and on." But Christy didn't—or wouldn't—go away. He campaigned for Trump. Not too effectively I would say. And he hung around until he eventually was given a role where he was dealing with staffing and personnel.

That might have seemed innocuous so some of the people in the campaign who figured, "How much harm can he do?"

But to me, the answer to that one was easy. A lot.

Christie was, to put it kindly, not just a squishy, liberal Republican. He was provably soft on Islam. When he was governor, he had appointed a member of the Muslim Brotherhood to a judgeship. And he had worked to prevent the deportation of a member of the Brotherhood who was unquestionably a threat. And, remember, the first plot to blow up the World Trade Towers was hatched in New Jersey.

I knew this and I was concerned enough about it that I wrote something to Steve Bannon. This was during the campaign and I don't know what Bannon did in the way of a follow-up. I do know that Christy only lasted a few days after the election. His staffing responsibilities were handed over to Mike Pence, the VP-elect and another soft Republican. Not as soft as Christy, maybe, but definitely someone whose instincts and loyalties all flowed in the direction of the old guard Republican party. The people, in other words, who Donald Trump had entered the campaign to oppose and so that he and people who thought the way he did could take over the Republican Party.

And those people were the very ones shut out of discussions about the new administration that was being put together. An administration that the people being ignored and passed over had made possible.

So we had that period after the election when Trump was up in the Tower, receiving visitors and we had the "golden elevator tour," with all these people going up to have an audience with him.

There was Henry Kissinger, the original "globalist," and you saw that and wondered, "What the hell is *he* doing up there?" And you have Leonardo DiCaprio who is not, to say the least, a MAGA guy. And you think, "What is he doing up there?" Then Al Gore gets on the golden elevator for his audience with Trump, so that they can talk about global warming. Bill Gates got an audience. And so on.

This was one more early warning sign of what the Trump administration would be dealing with now, when he took office, and maybe even for the duration of his first term and, perhaps, his entire presidency.

To the people who had been in the fight early, even from the beginning, it was discouraging to say the least. But it was increasingly clear that the RNC had taken over the transition and that the influence of the MAGA folks was diminishing.

I communicated my concerns to Bannon. I named names and tried to make the argument that personnel decisions were going to drive policy.

I think Bannon pretty clearly came around to my view. Eventually. His remarks on "60 Minutes," about how these staffing decisions were the "original sin of the administration," were right on point.

Just too late.

If the resistance had been fierce before Trump's victory, it became even more determined and ferocious after he was elected and then took office.

Some of this resistance was open and obvious and some, famously, was not. It wasn't until later that we would learn about the FBI and "Crossfire Hurricane." (And I'll get to that.) But long before then, it was obvious that there was a campaign of resistance conducted by people who, notionally, should have been Trump's allies. They were Republicans and they had a strong interest in the staffing of the administration.

Trump, who was coming from the outside—the far outside—didn't know where to go to find the people he needed to staff his administration. He was coming from another world. As a result, he made what I believe was the largest mistake of his administration and he made it even before he was sworn in to office.

He left it to the Republican establishment—particularly the Republican National Committee—to bring in people for positions in the administration. He got recommendations that he appoint this or that housebroken Republican to this or that position. And a lot of these people were not supporters and they did not necessarily buy into the Trump agenda. They would have been happier working for Jeb Bush and once they were on the job, it showed. They looked out for their own networks and self-interests. Jockeying for plumb jobs took priority over MAGA.

Then there were cases where the anti-Trump people on the RNC and elsewhere didn't simply push their own candidate for a position but actively worked to block someone they found unacceptable. Someone like…well, like me.

Before the election, some time back in the summer, I'd had some discussions with General Mike Flynn who was advising Trump on national security and would almost certainly be made head of the National Security Council when Trump won the election. Even though he was running behind in the polls at the time, and it seemed like every day there was another brush fire that had to be put out, they were saying "when" he'd won the election. Not "if."

These were the real Trump supporters and insurgents. They were, most definitely, not conventional Chamber of Commerce Republicans sensing a return to the good old days when someone named "Bush" was in the White House and the status quo was safe from disruption.

When the unthinkable happened and Trump was elected, General Mike Flynn said, I would be appointed as one of his senior deputies on the NSC as the Senior Director for Counterterrorism, a position formerly held by John Brennan. That job meant I would have access to the President. It was a place at the head table. Which, after all the years of trying to make my voice heard, with only limited success, sounded very good to me. Trump had run a "change" campaign and in the world of counterterrorism, if I was about anything at all, it was change.

But right away, it was chaos time.

Because Trump didn't have any experience with Washington and government, he didn't have people who have networks and know who would be a good fit, ideologically, politically and tem- peramentally with the President. He had to go to people for help.

Unbelievably, he went to the Republican National Committee. These were the people who now felt threatened. They felt, correctly, that they were losing their grip on power and influence in Washington. Losing it to people – like me – who considered themselves insurgents and wanted real change. Wanted, for instance, to end a war that the establishment Republicans had started and had no plan for winning. No plan at all, in fact, except continuing with what had been failing for fifteen years. Spending more and more money and sending more and more American kids to fight and die.

But if they could seed the Trump administration with their kind of people, that would be a way of cutting their losses until there was another election and the status quo ante could be restored. Think of it as a sort of holding operation for the Deep State.

There were active saboteurs as well. NeverTrump individuals with Bush, Romney and McCain that had infiltrated the transition. Folks like Bill Hagerty from Tennessee, who had been an executive in Jeb Bush's Tennessee campaign and had strong ties with Islamic finance networks. Others like John Gallagher, who entered the transition through John McCain's staff and who told a colleague during an interview, "Maybe I was placed inside the transition to sabotage his administration" or words to that effect. Bannon booted Gallagher from the transition, but it wasn't until close to the Inauguration and at that point the damage was done. The people Gallagher and Hagerty had helped place were already inside.

So when Steve Bannon went to the Conservative Political Action Conference (CPAC) and said "If you think they're going to give us our country back without a fight, you're sadly mistaken..." he was absolutely right. And that was only a month after Trump's inauguration.

Not quite a year after the election—sometime in October of 2017—Steven Bannon appeared on "Sixty Minutes." Bannon had been the chief executive officer of the campaign and he had been the chief strategist for the administration for a little less than nine months. Trump fired him, partly because he got too much media attention but mainly because he was a lightning rod for criticism. Especially from people who would never be Trump's allies.

Go figure.

Steve is smart and he has a brain that is tuned like a seismograph to the shifting of political realities. Which is why he saw the coming of the populist wave long before the establishment media, which probably couldn't have defined the word.

And Bannon was smart enough to know, when he sat down for his "Sixty Minutes" interview, that things were going wrong for the Trump administration, in spite of the good economy and all of the rest of it, and that there was a reason. It was because, in Steve's words, "'The Republican establishment is trying to nullify the 2016 election."

Trump's original sin, as he said, was in thinking that he could cut a deal with the Republican establishment. Trump had turned to the RNC when he needed to staff his administration. And the RNC took the opportunity to blackball Trump supporters and bring in its kind of people. McCain people. Bush people. Romney people. The RNC created a website where people who wanted to work in the administration could send their resumés. But it didn't bring in a single person who had applied. On staffing, the neocons, Never-Trump, and the Republican establishment just ran the table. Even Democrats managed to break through the hiring process, but very few, if any, from the MAGA crowd.

The administration still has not completely recovered.

Particularly in the area of foreign policy.

One of the things we'd always say in the operations world, the EOD world, is if an operation starts badly, you'll spend 90% of the rest of the effort trying to get it back on track. So the EOD motto for all explosive specialists, like me, on our patches and stuff, is "Initial success or total failure." And when I think about Trump, I think about how he missed that mark. Having won the election, he assumed he could just walk into the presidency, not realizing that politics is a 24/7 contact sport. And winning the election? Sure, you won it. For about 30 seconds, and then you're on to your re-election. I mean, it's hard for people that aren't in politics to understand that.

Trump began his Presidency in a hole that had been dug by the RNC. He might have thought he was digging himself out but he was just digging deeper.

And the most distressing part is that even when things started to go wrong, he didn't understand why and he didn't change. He kept going to the same old roster of conventional old political hacks from the permanent Washington establishment.

There was, for instance, the man hired, then fired, as his national security advisor. His _second_ National Security Advisor, or third, if you count Mike Flynn, who didn't last long enough to learn his way around the Executive Office Building where his office was.

John Bolton had replaced H.R. McMaster and I'll get to him later. The point I want to make here is that Bolton is a paid-up member of the Washington foreign policy establishment and political class. He is a neo-con in good standing and there is no evidence on his record that he would be in favor of doing what Trump had promised to do in his campaign—namely, get us out of those wars that we could not seem to either win or end.

This was right there in plain sight and anyone who looked at Bolton's record could see it.

It was no secret who John Bolton was. It's probably on his business cards. _John Bolton, Neocon Extraordinaire._ The man probably _still_ believes there are weapons of mass destruction hidden in Iraq.

Well, Trump finally got rid of Bolton because he kind of sensed that he was sabotaging some of his initiatives. And the one that really was bothering the President was that Bolton was seen as a saboteur of his North Korea initiatives. People have told me that Bolton was pushing the Gaddafi route with Trump. Bolton publicly stated so. So we have the one guy who did give up his nuclear program and what did it get him? We launched an operation that resulted in him getting shot in the head, thrown in a ditch, and pissed on. Recall Hillary Clinton cackling, "We came, we saw, he died."

Very funny and certainly how you would like to come off when you are trying to persuade rogue regimes to give up nuclear weapons or, if they don't have them already, to stop trying to develop them.

Bolton is a chicken hawk who did some time in the Maryland National Guard during Vietnam, but he largely avoided the war. He's a total advocate of the neo-con regime-change agenda that depends on using American troops to fight wars that can't be won unless we start killing a lot more people than we've been willing to kill, up until now. Kill 500,000 people, even five million and maybe you could pacify Afghanistan. Kill 50,000 and you get what we've got. Eighteen years of fighting, casualties, stalemate, and no end in sight.

In his heart, Trump wants no part of that. Trump is a foreign policy realist. The question is...why did he appoint Bolton in the first place?

THE MEMO CONTINUED Far from politics as usual, this is a political warfare effort that seeks the destruction of a sitting president.

Since Trump took office, the situation has intensified to crisis level proportions. For those engaged in the effort, especially those from within the Deep State or permanent government apparatus, this raises clear Title 18 (legal) concerns.

15

INTO THE HEART OF THE RESISTANCE: THE NSC

As I wrote earlier, I'd had some conversations—I suppose you would characterize them as "casual" —during the campaign, with General Flynn and Steve Bannon about my coming to work for the administration. Flynn would be head of the National Security Council and I would be working for him in some fairly senior capacity. The logical area of my responsibilities would, of course, be counterterrorism. That's what I knew and where I had worked.

After the election, Flynn and I communicated five or six times by phone and e-mail. A former Navy SEAL friend of mine who had worked on the campaign continued to nudge my name in front of Flynn and Bannon. I would send Flynn something when I thought it would be useful to him, or he could use a heads-up, and he would respond. We were in touch but not on a daily basis or anything.

Then, toward the end of December, we had a conversation. It was the 29th. I remember because it was my Dad's birthday, I got a call from Flynn to confirm what had so far been talked about in a sort of casual, offhand fashion. I was going to be on the NSC and my title would be Counterterrorism Senior Director and Special Assistant to the President, which meant I would have access to Trump. This was John Brennan's old job.

This was an opportunity to really make a difference, to change things and get out of the rut that we were in that had been dug by previous administrations, Republican and Democrat.

"Okay," I said. Eagerly.

After a little time had passed—less than two weeks—I got another call. My appointment to the NSC wasn't happening. I was out.

I didn't have to do a lot of snooping around to find out what had happened to change things. There were some people in the NSC who'd been throwing up some chaff. One of them was especially well connected in the D.C. insider culture. His name was Mustafa Javed Ali. He was the prototypical Deep State player. He had worked at the Defense Intelligence Agency, the Department of Homeland Security, and the Federal Bureau of Investigation. Along with assignments to the National Intelligence Council, the National Counterterrorism Center and, finally,. the National Security Council where he made sure I didn't get in at a level where I might be a threat to the "Islam is not the issue" narrative.

He stayed busy putting down such threats because he saw lots of them. Mostly in the form of Trump people.

He had influence but nobody could quite say why. Supposedly, he spoke for the moderate "Islam is a religion of peace" position and was someone to whom attention needed to be paid. He knew my reputation as someone who was unsentimental when it came to Islam.

He and others leaned on Preibus and Flynn to veto my appointment to the NSC. I'd known something was up when the calls stopped coming from the people I expected I would be working with after the inauguration. And my own calls were not being returned. Always a sure sign of something that could not be good.

Finally, eight or nine days after the call saying I had the job, I got the one that said, "Well, not so fast. Sorry."

They didn't want someone on the NSC who was known to take a hard line on Islam. Who was, in other words, a realist.

I was disappointed, obviously. And maybe a little surprised, at first. But this changed as I learned more about what was going on at the White House. Which was an absolute bloodbath.

The Inauguration came and went, but I continued to work my campaign contacts and managed to finally break through on February 10, when I received the offer of a position on the NSC, but much lower down on the totem pole.

Flynn was out the following week and was looking at criminal charges for lying to the FBI. It wasn't until much later that it became clear he'd been set up, by Andrew McCabe who was acting FBI Director at the time and was eventually fired for—wait for it—lying to the FBI.

Interestingly, back during the transition, I had sent a memo to a prominent conservative close to the administration, listing some of the people the Trump administration needed to go after. These were people who were total enemies of Trump and could be counted on to do whatever they could to frustrate him, handcuff him—literally, if possible—and, one way or another, drive him out of the White

House and Washington, which they considered their turf. The name at the top of the list I sent was … Andrew McCabe.

There were other interesting names on the list. Including James Clapper, the Director of National Intelligence. He would become one of Trump's fiercest enemies. What always interested me about this is that he comes out of the intelligence community where people are supposed to guard their anonymity and stay back in the shadows. Clapper never seems to have trouble finding a platform or cable news interviewer eager to hear him go off on Trump.

The departure of Flynn (and I'll have more on that later) just added to the general sense of chaos surrounding the staffing of the new administration. Bannon was trying to get the Trump loyalists in but he was up against the heavy influence of the RNC old hands and insiders. It wasn't even a fair fight. The man who was picked to replace Flynn, General H. R. McMaster, was a pure pedigreed Washington insider, on record publicly declaring that the "Islamic State is not Islamic," and the jihadists were "really irreligious organizations." Those lines came from a speech he gave in 2014 when he also said that the jihadists were not motivated by religion but by "fear" and a "sense of honor." And, that the U.S. had to begin "understanding those human dimensions."

ISIS as a secular movement, then. No need to understand its Islamic roots. Never mind that the self-proclaimed Islamic State was started and led by a man with a PhD in Islamic Studies from Baghdad University.

Trump had only been President for a few weeks and that's how far, when it came to personnel, the White House had traveled down the old road back to fighting the "war on terror." To buying into the narrative and denying reality.

In early February, I was approached about coming in at a much more junior level than the one I had basically accepted earlier and in a role that was not in counterterrorism. This new role would have me working strategic planning, which I could do, even though it wasn't exactly playing to my strength or maximizing my experience and capabilities. Also, on top of everything else, I would be making less money. Not just less than I was currently making in the private sector but less than I had been making in my last government job when I was still with the DoD.

It was almost like they wanted to insult me into saying "no." They would low ball me and basically make an offer that it would be real easy to take as an insult and refuse and just go away.

There was part of me that wanted to do exactly that.

I didn't need this, I told myself. I'd been with the Trump campaign when it was treated as a joke by the national media and the Washington crowd. I had been working counterterrorism and studying Islam and devoting my life to this world ever since 9/11. Since before that, actually, all the way back to when I was an EOD bomb guy at the White House. This was the world I knew and lived in and where I had something to contribute. Make a difference. Do something important.

All of that.

It would have made me feel good – maybe for a minute – to tell them to take their job and shove it.

But this was too big a decision to make just on emotion.

So, I talked it over with my family and some friends.

Most of them told me to hang back, wait a couple of years and see if things didn't change and open up for people like me. Which is to say … the real Trump people. Those who had been with him since even before he won the nomination and when the conventional wisdom was that he had no chance. The people who were there for something larger than their own career ambitions.

I listened to that advice, took it seriously, and thought about it. It made sense from a career standpoint.

But going in, even in a position that was junior to my experience and other qualifications, meant that I would be part of the first wave. As a Special Forces colonel working counterterrorism at the Pentagon told me...the early days of the Trump administration would set the tone and establish the precedents...the ones I would be following and otherwise dealing with if I waited and came in later.

So, I did some negotiating and got my pay up close to where it should have been. It still meant I would be a mid-level staffer who did not have direct access to the head of the NSC and, hence, the President. People wouldn't be coming to me on the big questions so I would have to make myself heard. Which was okay since I had experience doing that.

And, then, I believed—and still do—that these were critical times for the United States of America. With Trump, there was still an opportunity to change course and avoid what could be a disaster. The jihadists weren't the only threat we were looking at. There was also China, which was eating our lunch economically while it was busy building a military that could challenge us in the Pacific. There would be serious pressure on Trump, applied by the Chamber of Commerce type of Republicans, to give in to China on just about everything. Their economic interests were far more important to the country club Republicans than any national security concerns.

And, then, there was immigration. In the same way they wanted to stay with the *status quo* when it came to China, they wanted to keep the flow of cheap labor that came into the U.S. in the form of immigration – legal and otherwise.

I made my decision to take the job on the NSC even though I knew, going in, that there were going to be people gunning for me. They had, after all, already shot me down once. They were not going to stop coming after me because I was on the inside.

To the contrary.

But I told myself what I had told people in the Trump campaign in the hours and days after the election. They were all celebrating and looking at the future like it was all going to be just one easy day after another. I didn't see it like that. In fact, I was thinking—well, actually, I *knew*—that from here on, things would just get harder.

Like I told the people doing the celebrating on Election night: we were in the first wave on the way into Omaha Beach. The real fight was still ahead of us.

THE MEMO CONTINUED Subversion undermines or detaches the loyalties of significant political and social groups within the target state and transfers political and/ or ideological loyalties to the counter-state. As the counter-state forms, a counter-elite of influential individual and key leaders within the target state will later facilitate the legitimacy and permanency of the new regime.

16

HITTING THE BEACH

Going back to the White House was a little strange. Like going back to the house where you had lived when you were a kid and seeing that it hadn't changed much at all. While, in the meantime, you had changed almost completely. Had grown up, in short, and gotten real.

When I went to get badged on my first day there, I was reminded of that kid who had been me twenty years earlier. They still had my name and my photograph in the system. The woman running the security badging office found that amusing.

This time around, I wasn't one of the guys supporting the Secret Service. I was one of the people being protected by them and my new job was strategic planning. I was part of a unit that was made up of a director and three of us who worked for him as planners. I did ideological warfare and focused on communism and Islam. One of the others did India. And the other was an expert on China. It was a sort of a hybrid group. We were what is called "disruptive thinkers."

Meaning we were supposed to be looking out over the horizon while most of the other people in the NSC were focused on the day to day. It was stimulating work and something I felt like I had been working my way up to for twenty years now; coming from the battlefield instead of the ivory towers. Unlike the think tank, wonky types, I'd gotten my education down in the trenches.

Well…there was that stretch in the National Defense University, but even that was close to the action.

My office was on the third floor of the Old Executive Office Building (OEOB) and it was nice enough for government quarters. There were the usual furnishings. Utilitarian desks and sturdy chairs. White board on two walls. TV always tuned to 24-hour news. Safes for securing classified documents. Secure telephones. Cell phones were, of course, not allowed. We each had a desk in one corner of the room and our boss had an office off to one side of the room. We were in a more or less central location in the building with the Middle East planners on one side of us; South America next to them. On the other side there was Counterterrorism. Like I say, it all felt very familiar and I had no complaints…except.

One day, I got a look at the office that would have been mine if I had gotten that first job I'd been recommended for: Counterterrorism Senior Director and Special Assistant to the President. That office was…well, *palatial.* No other word for it. Very big with tall ceilings, windows, and a view. Bookshelves and paintings. And, most of all, a twenty-person conference table. It had once been the Secretary of War's office.

The mood around the White House and the OEOB was serious, the way it is in most government offices. You are there to do important work and, of course, some people would take this a little too far and get puffed up and self-important. Especially if they had never worked in the White House—or even Washington—before.

There was not much to laugh about at the NSC. Though it was, in some sense, a joke. Just not the funny kind.

Within a couple of days of my starting there, I realized that the place was staffed, largely anyways, with legacy personnel from the Obama administration. They were technically "holdovers." But it was pretty clear that they weren't planning on going any place and there was nobody around with any interest in getting rid of them in order to make room for people appointed by Trump. People who would be, therefore, loyal to his MAGA agenda.

Which the holdovers most definitely were not.

Instead of being committed to advancing the President's agenda, they were determined to sabotage it. And they evidently didn't care who knew it. I caught on to it right away.

In fact, one of the first encounters I had there was with a young man who later became famous—I suppose you could say—as the anonymous "whistleblower" in the Trump impeachment proceedings. His name, by the way, is Eric Ciaramella. He was an Agency analyst before and after he was at the NSC and he is one of John Brennan's little elves. He was right out front about his loyalties... or lack of same. He was overheard, shortly after Trump took office, talking about how he and the others were going to "get rid of" Flynn and the President. He was on a list a couple of my insurgent colleagues and I put together. We had identified him as the first person who needed to be removed from the NSC.

But he was just one of many. There were others. One of them had been Ben Rhodes' assistant when he was Deputy to Obama's National Security Advisor, Susan Rice. Another was a Clinton Fellow named Fernando Cutz. And there were many more. The NSC was crawling with them.

Against six or seven of us MAGA types.

It was, to say the very least, a strange dynamic. We were people who believed in the President's agenda and were working to advance it. They were unalterably opposed to him and wanted to sabotage that agenda.

But we were the ones who were outnumbered and playing defense.

It seemed counterintuitive at best, insane at worst.

But there it was.

Things might have been different if General Flynn had been in charge. But he was out and facing federal charges for lying to the FBI. James Comey, who was still Director of the Bureau, had set him up.

Here's how it worked:

The FBI had transcripts of a conversation between Flynn and the Russian ambassador over an unsecured line. This was during the period between the election and the Inauguration. Trump was putting his administration together and Flynn would be his National Security Advisor.

The call concerned sanctions put in place by President Obama during his last month in office. It was the sort of thing that the incoming National Security Advisor and the Russian Ambassador to the United States would be expected to talk about. And since Flynn was vacationing in the Dominican Republic at the time, the conversation was held over an unsecured line. The FBI listened in and made transcripts. There was never any mystery about what Flynn and the ambassador discussed. The FBI merely had to read the transcripts.

And there was nothing illegal or unethical or, even, unseemly about the conversation. Flynn was doing his job and probably not happy about having to interrupt his vacation to do it. Still …

After the Inauguration, with Flynn in his White House office for just a few days, Comey decided that someone needed to call him and say there are some things about his conversation with the Russian ambassador that need to be cleared up. Just a few loose hanging threads, General. Routine Bureau business.

Which, if Flynn had been paying attention, would have set off all the alarm bells and sirens.

And he would have been on total red alert when he saw the call hadn't gone through the White House Counsel's office and that nobody was advising him that he might want to have a lawyer in the room with him. This was Comey's idea and his way of setting Flynn up. And Flynn, who was busy and no doubt distracted, fell for it.

Comey even bragged, later on, about how he had orchestrated the whole scheme, describing it as "…something I probably wouldn't have done or wouldn't have gotten away with in a more organized administration. In the George W. Bush Administration or the Obama Administration, if the FBI wanted to send agents into the White House to interview a senior official, you would work through the White House counsel, there would be discussions and approvals [about] who would be there. And I thought, it's early enough let's just send a couple guys over."

On Comey's instructions, Andrew McCabe, the Deputy Director of the Bureau made the call and said to Flynn that, he "… thought the quickest way to get this done was to have a conversation between [Mr. Flynn] and the agents only. I further stated that if General Flynn wished to include anyone else in the meeting, like the White House Counsel for instance, that I would need to involve the Department of Justice. [Mr. Flynn] stated that this would not be necessary and agreed to meet with the agents without any additional participants."

Flynn was collegial. McCabe was devious.

Flynn was co-operating in his own execution.

He sat down with the agents who, when they wrote up their account of the conversation in what the Bureau calls a "Form 302," reported that Flynn had been "...relaxed and jocular" and "clearly saw the FBI agents as allies."

One of those two agents, by the way, was Peter Strzok. He later became famous for the texts he exchanged with his mistress, Lisa Page, an FBI lawyer who worked for McCabe. In one of those texts, he famously described how he "Just went to a southern Virginia Wal-Mart...[where he] could SMELL the Trump support."

Like his boss, McCabe, Strzok was eventually fired from the FBI. So was his lover, Lisa Page.

But that was long after Strzok had interviewed Flynn and, with his partner, written up that 302 that pretty much said Flynn is telling the truth. But this wasn't the conclusion McCabe was looking for. He wanted that 302 rewritten to say, essentially, that Flynn was lying. So he supposedly had Peter Strzok and the other case agent revise their 302 form and had Ms. Page, McCabe's lawyer, ensure it met the requisite threshold of illegality. It wasn't the only time that someone in the FBI had lied that way. FBI Lawyer Kevin Clinesmith, a co-worker of theirs, would later be fired for altering CIA documents about Dr. Carter Page in order to create a false justification for Foreign Intelligence Surveillance Act (FISA) surveillance against Page.

Now, with the rewritten 302 as ammunition, the FBI came down hard and went to Vice-President Pence with the evidence that

Flynn had been lying in his interview. The evidence was, of course, those altered 302s. Flynn had previously assured the VP that he had told the truth. Pence told Flynn that after he and his wife had prayed for guidance and slept on the news, they had decided they could not "forgive" Flynn.

Pence, by now, is the personnel guy in the White House and since Flynn no longer has his support, he does the honorable thing and resigns. He is later indicted and pleads guilty. He does this to a) avoid personal financial ruin and b) to protect his son who was vulnerable to one of those scorched earth investigations by the FBI and the IRS and any other government agency that could make his life a living hell.

Years later, when the news eventually comes out about the fraudulent 302, and the rest of it, Flynn withdraws his plea.

Now at the time, the FBI seemed to be going to an awful lot of trouble just to get rid of Mike Flynn. Not to mention running the risks of being exposed. Why, you had to wonder, was it so important to the FBI that Mike Flynn get booted from the NSC.

The default explanation was simple. The Deep State needed Flynn gone because he was a threat to the status quo. If he and his team stayed, then that would work to advance the implementation of the Trump foreign policy agenda. There might be an audit of the Intelligence Community or some systemic changes. We might even get out of Afghanistan and Iraq. Get tougher with China. All of it.

So, in this version, getting rid of Flynn was just political hardball. Very hard. And very dirty. But nothing that Washington hadn't seen before.

So carry on.

And, as it turned out, things worked out fine for the people who wanted Flynn gone for policy reasons. The NSC did nothing to implement Trump's policies under his replacement and just about everything it could to sidetrack them. It became an obstacle to the agenda that Trump had run on and that had gotten him elected. So the obvious, pedestrian explanation for the takedown of Flynn seems to be correct. But there was more to it. So much more.

It all went back to an illegal FBI operation—and you might even call it a Deep State conspiracy—which the Bureau had counted on remaining secret when Hillary Clinton was elected and which it was now in a panic to keep from being exposed.

And I'll come to that.

But first...at the NSC, we got a new boss. Lieutenant General H.R. McMaster.

Before I went to work for him, I was inclined to think of McMaster as potentially one of the good guys. This was based mostly on his book, ***Dereliction of Duty***: *Johnson, McNamara, the Joint Chiefs of Staff, and the Lies That Led to Vietnam.*

That title lays out the book's thesis pretty clearly. McMaster made the case that the war wasn't lost in the rice paddies and the jungles of Vietnam, but in the bureaucratic corridors and offices of Washington. In the White House and the Pentagon, where people went from lying to the public to lying to themselves. Where they came up with a strategy that wasn't designed to win the war, but, instead, to not lose it. And to keep the American voters, whose sons were being drafted to go off and fight and die in Vietnam, in the dark about what was going on in the war and what it would take to fight it to win.

The book's genesis was in the early 1990s, as McMaster's PhD thesis at the University of North Carolina. He was an army major at the time. The book was commercially published in 1997 and became something of a required reading in the Pentagon among an officers corps that was determined not to make those mistakes again.

The thinking was that if McMaster—who had risen to the rank of Lieutenant General—had gotten it right about Vietnam, then surely he would get it right about our current un-winnable wars in the mid-East and Afghanistan. Especially since he had served in both and would have experienced the problems and frustrations up close and personal.

Well, this was the glass half full way of looking at it.

The glass half empty approach was to study his career since he had left the military. From 2006-2017, McMaster served as a fellow at the International Institute of Strategic Studies (IISS). The IISS is another one of those globalist think tanks, funded by George Soros and multiple foreign governments, including $25 million from the Bahraini royal family. They are a dime a dozen and they exist solely to push the globalist worldview which means never ending wars, hostility with Russia and regime change from Libya to Venezuela.

I have seen this playbook before. A military officer drinks the globalist Kool-Aid in order to rise up the ranks and then, upon retirement, is promptly rewarded with think tank fellowships and board seats at military contractors.

I was hopeful but I feared the globalists had gotten to McMaster. I was right.

With Flynn out, McMaster was my boss when I went to work at the NSC. But I never met with him. He never called me into his office to tell me the usual stuff about how he was glad to have me on the team. Which seemed a little strange at the time. There were not so many people on the NSC staff that he couldn't have taken the time to welcome me aboard and give me the pep talk about how we were there to serve the President and the country and do big things and so on and so forth.

I realized later that, since I had been backed by Bannon and other MAGA folks for the job and had been friendly with Flynn, McMaster may have believed I was going to be a problem. Anyways, I was now so far down on the totem pole that it didn't matter to him. There was no point in cordiality.

And, of course, he was right, on both counts. I was a problem because I believed my job was to serve the President and his agenda, and I was too far down on the totem pole to have any direct impact with the President. Anyway, there were far more disconcerting aspects to life in the NSC than the remoteness of the leadership. There was, above all, an outright resistance to the Trump agenda, right across the board.

When the President made his desires known on, for instance, getting out of Afghanistan, the people in the NSC made it their business not to come up with plans for implementing the policy but to make the argument for why things the President wanted done could not be done. And to obstruct their implementation.

If you talked to them about a troop withdrawal and said that we could keep eyes on Afghanistan with satellites and drones and do what we needed to do with air-power and quick, in-and-out strikes by spec ops they would come back with, "Oh, no. That's just too dangerous…it's a non-starter. You know, ISIS will come back and, you know, al Qaeda is already back."

Which was pretty much the point. Our just being there wasn't getting it done and there was no way we were ever going to send in enough troops to get it done. We weren't prepared to kill a million Afghans in order to win. Which meant…we were going to lose.

"Okay, then," you would say, "what is *your* plan forward?"

And you would get this word fog that amounted to…*nothing*. Just a "plan" to muddle on forever.

And you would say, "Okay. Say we stay. Just keep on, keeping on. How are you going to deal with the corruption issues there? How are you going to deal with the fact they have no good central government? How are you gonna deal with the fact the Taliban now controls more territory than they did in September of 2001? And what about the 'green-on-blue' attacks—where Afghan soldiers are intentionally attacking and killing U.S. soldiers? You know, where do you see this *ending*?"

Well, you would be told, the consensus was we could *not* just get out.

And this is what would bubble up to McMaster, who seemed to think that his role was to tell the President what the government institutions would agree to do and communicate that to the President.

The thing was inverted. Upside down. The bureaucracy was telling the President what it was willing to do and not do.

I believe that the holdovers wanted us to stay in Afghanistan because it had been their boss, Obama, who had surged the troops and made nation- building the central mission. Leaving would go into the Obama record book as an **L.** And this was insupportable.

As for McMaster…as time went on, it became clear that he was on his way to becoming what the people he had written about so forcefully in his book — an apologist for a failed strategy and a hopeless war.

When the staff of the NSC was not obstructing on policy—which it did pretty much full time—it was working the old party line about Islam and how the <u>*real danger*</u> was not Muslim terrorists who believed they were doing Allah's will as received by Mohammed, but rather an infection of the American body politic by some bacillus of anti-Muslim bigotry.

It was so old and so out of synch with Trump and what he had been elected to do that it was hard to believe. It almost made you tired. It was like we were not merely a continuation of the Obama administration but had retreated all the way back to Bush and the "Islam is a religion of peace" line. Hard for some of us to believe—or accept—but that's how it was and it showed itself in all sorts of ways.

There was the time, for instance, when a woman named Ayaan Hirsi Ali had been invited to come to our offices and deliver a talk on Islamic terror.

Her credentials were certainly in order. Born in Somalia, to Muslim parents, she had undergone the rituals of female genital mutilation and forced marriage as a young girl before she fled to the Netherlands where she got a university education and became a member of Parliament and a critic of Dutch immigration policies which, she argued, were too accommodating, especially to Muslims who showed no potential for assimilation.

She eventually collaborated with filmmaker Theo van Gogh on a film called *Submission,* which was a very tough indictment of the way Islam legitimized the brutal and abusive treatment of women. The film was, needless to say, very controversial and, not long after it was released, van Gogh was murdered by a jihadist. A letter calling for the death of Hirsi Ali was stuck on his body, pinned there by a knife.

Hirsi Ali left Europe for the United States where she became a citizen and, among other things, a fellow at both at the American

Enterprise Institute and the Hoover Institute. She has written several important books. In those books, and in her lectures, she forcefully makes the case that Islam is fundamentally antagonistic to Western values and that it is a special threat to women.

She is a serious scholar and she has her own real-life experiences for backup. You would think that she would be someone that the people at the NSC would be eager to hear speak. So, of course, McMaster and Mustafa Javed Ali prohibited her from speaking unless there was someone appearing with her to refute what she was saying. Equal time, you see. In the name of *"fairness."*

Mustafa Javed Ali, who had torpedoed my appointment for the job he now held—Senior Director of Counterterrorism—was the likely manipulator in this whole, sorry episode. And that's the way things ran with McMaster in charge. Ayaan Hirsi Ali did meet privately with the group of 6-7 Trump supporters, but nobody else was allowed to hear from her.

The few of us who were in opposition to the mood and the actions of the NSC—who were, that is, loyal to the President—had conversations among ourselves. We weren't exactly a cabal. But we knew we were outnumbered and that we couldn't give the leadership any excuse for getting rid of us. But we knew *something had to be done.* Starting with the personnel question. If the NSC were ever to operate in the interests of Trump's agenda on foreign policy, then it had to be staffed with people who believed in that agenda.

Very simple, you'd think. But this was war, of a sort, and as von Clausewitz famously wrote, "Everything in war is very simple, but the simplest thing is difficult."

And if this wasn't war, exactly, it was certainly politics, of a sort. And so, could be a reverse of another of those famous Clausewitz aphorisms: "War is the continuation of politics by other means." ...

The few of us at NSC who were loyal to Trump began drawing up a list of people who we *knew* had to be run out of the building. And we found a way to get the list into the hands of people we thought might be able to take action on it. People like Jared Kushner and Steve Bannon.

Well, McMaster got wind of what we were doing. He called an all-hands meeting and stood in front of the room and said, in effect, "There are no 'holdovers.' We are all on the same team."

He was looking directly at me when he said it.

This was not, of course, the way to solve policy issues. It wasn't a question of overcoming interoffice political squabbles and getting everybody to pull together for the good of the team. There were serious issues and hard, deep disagreements at work. Some of us also believed that we were dealing with people who were busy subverting the President and his policies.

They weren't going to be talked out of what they believed. And those of us who wanted them gone weren't going to be teaming up with them for the sake of the greater good.

I was frustrated and alarmed. I saw the opportunity that had come with Trump's election slipping away. So I started work on a project that I hoped would sound the alarm and result in change.

But first...back to the firing of General Flynn.

The few of us at the NSC who were not Obama holdovers, and were still loyal to Trump, believed that things would have been different if Flynn had not been forced to resign over the FBI's trap.

He would never have been a pliable tool of the holdovers the way McMaster was. Flynn would probably have cleaned house.

Still, the question in the minds of many of us was...why had the FBI gone to such great lengths to catch Flynn in a "lie"? If, that is, he had really been lying.

In the world that my fellow insurgents and I lived and worked in, you hear rumors and you develop sources. People with security clearances are still people and you hear gossip. Some of what you hear is even true. A lot of it never makes the news. Some of it just goes away if there is nobody to bring the story public and make enough people—the right people—pay attention and take action.

I had friends who were FBI and CIA and DoD. And even back during the campaign, some of them were giving me these cryptic warnings. "Something is going on," someone would say. "It might even be an Op." Not just the usual Washington leaks, then, which are sort of passive in nature. People who know things that they should and are telling people they shouldn't. What I was hearing, by inference, was that people were doing things they shouldn't, to learn things they shouldn't know. And then using that information for their own (possibly political) reasons. What I was hearing had, like I say, more substance than the usual rumor and gossip, but it didn't rise to the actionable level. Still...it was more than Washington static noise.

So you think the usual things. Maybe there is a mole. But we already knew that. There were these leaks to the media that were happening almost daily.

But this had the feel of something a lot bigger than one person with access and an axe to grind.

Well, among the things my colleagues did at NSC was auditing various sources of intelligence. To include the monitoring of electronic communications under the FISA. And, in doing this, one of them came across the records of phone surveillance that had been going on for months now. Since before the election. And what my colleague discovered was that...*it was perhaps still going on, now, several months after the election and that it was not merely "widespread," but included surveillance of the President, himself. The FBI had been spying on Trump since before he was nominated and may be spying on him still.* Not only were they spying on him, but also, they were spying on the entire Trump campaign and "unmasking" or revealing the names of American citizens involved in those conversations.

It was part of an FBI op with the code name "Crossfire Hurricane."

THE MEMO CONTINUED The recent turn of events give rise to the observation that the defense of President Trump is the defense of America.

In the same way President Lincoln was surrounded by political opposition both inside and outside of his wire, in both overt and covert forms, so too is President Trump. Had Lincoln failed, so too would have the Republic.

17

A FIGHTING
WITHDRAWAL

My fellow MAGA insurgents and I at the NSC didn't know it at the time, but we were present, active, and, in a real sense, responsible for getting the ball rolling in exposing the greatest political scandal in American history of the United States. This scandal is still unfolding as I write, and it will likely be a long time before all the details have been fully aired and the whole truth is known.

But what we had already learned by early 2020 is staggering enough: that working in concert, elements of the FBI, and CIA, highly placed holdovers from the Obama administration, members of the media, and others, used the machinery of the government—especially the national security component—to first seek to prevent the election of Donald Trump and, once he had nonetheless been elected, to drive him from office.

Among the schemes the plotters discussed were secretly recording the President and using the 25th Amendment to get the cabinet to remove the President from office; a move that would have required that the "Vice President and a majority of either the principal officers of the executive departments…transmit to the House and Senate… their written declaration that the President is unable to discharge the powers and duties of his office…." This plot was abandoned in the planning stages.

The President's enemies failed again to overturn the outcome of the 2016 election, spectacularly so. When the protracted Special Counsel investigation turned up no evidence of what the media routinely and willfully called "collusion" with the Russians the House Democratic majority immediately drew up Articles of Impeachment, based wholly upon a fraudulent IG claim by the Obama holdover Eric Ciaramella. The vote was strictly along party lines, albeit with a few Democrats defecting and one appalled Congressman changing his party membership from Democrat to Republican.

All of these failed efforts made increasingly clear the desperation of the opposition composed of Deep Staters of both parties to overturn the results of the 2016 election. And, not incidentally, to cover up its own crimes, committed in that attempt, as well as multiple other instances of their own corruption.

As I wrote earlier, those of us at the NSC who were Trump loyalists – and, hence, a minority were suspicious from the onset that *something* was going on. It was quickly apparent that the obstruction and the subversion of Trump and his agenda at hand was more than just normal Washington politics at play. There was just too much in the way of outright sabotage; from efforts to embarrass the President that could only have come from close to the top, to the sorts of leaks of phone conversations between the president and leaders of other nations that would have been unimaginable in the Bush or Obama administrations.

There were clearly anti-Trump plants and moles everywhere in the administration. And individuals conducting illegal, electronic surveillance.

Which brings me back to General Flynn and his resignation and his troubles very early on with the FBI.

Why, people wondered at the time, was the FBI so clearly interested in Flynn and so plainly eager to get him out as head of the NSC? Indeed, so eager, we were to learn much later, that senior FBI leadership had ordered the reports proving Flynn innocent of lying to agents in his White House interview be rewritten to prove his guilt.

Why was getting rid of Flynn *that* important?

Well, it wasn't that he knew too much—yet. It was that he might *learn* too much.

For the same reason, Jeff Sessions had been compelled during his Senate confirmation process to recuse himself from anything pertaining to Russia. He also, it was feared, might learn too much.

Might learn, in short, about the operation that the FBI called "Crossfire Hurricane."

Much has been written about CH. And there will be many more volumes to come. And I don't propose to review it all here. I'll get to that in another book. Suffice it to say, that CH began as a joint intelligence operation into supposed collusion between the Russian government and the Trump campaign and that it expanded, after Trump's inauguration, into a campaign to remove the President of the United States. This operation was conducted by corrupt agents of the FBI and DOJ and augmented by other elements of the Intelligence Community. Which is to say...the United States government.

So, call it what it was...an attempted coup.

It was fueled, first, by a fierce opposition to Trump and a desire to keep him from being elected. And, then, once he had been, to get enough goods on him to drive him from office; and, if they could not be found, to invent some. By the end, this had become a matter of desperate self-preservation; so much so, that it led to a sham IG complaint used to gin up the most partisan impeachment in the history of the United States.

An essential tool throughout this effort was electronic surveillance. It began long before the publicly acknowledged date of July 2016, when, following Trump's nomination, the FBI went to the Foreign Surveillance Intelligence Court to ask for warrants to eavesdrop on people connected with his campaign.

Even these warrants, obtained on the flimsiest of grounds, by law had to be periodically renewed; and the grounds became more flimsy until, in June 2017, the FBI was reduced to flatly lying in the applications. In the FBI's application for a fourth warrant on its subject, Carter Page, the FBI was required by law to cite any cooperation with law enforcement by the subject. The FBI had possession of an e-mail detailing Page's cooperation with the CIA. An FBI lawyer named Kevin Clinesmith simply rewrote the document so that it now asserted the opposite. Namely, there was no such relationship. The Inspector General of the Justice Department, Horowitz, has since recommended that Clinesmith be criminally prosecuted.

But that was just one lie among many.

When it needed to persuade the FISA court to issue a warrant, the FBI famously relied on what came to be known as the "Steele Dossier." Indeed, this document was as essential to the criminal fraud of "Crossfire Hurricane" as the *"secret file"* had been to the Dreyfus case. It was the big lie that held the thing together.

The "Steele Dossier" was a piece of opposition research done by a former British spy. It was paid for by the Clinton campaign and it purported to prove corrupt entanglements between Trump and the Russian government, including efforts to sabotage the 2016 election. For a sweetener, there was even some kinky stuff about Russian hookers being paid to urinate on a bed that had once been slept in by Barrack Obama. With Trump, of course, watching this depraved exhibition.

All this was just too good for the FBI and much of the American media which, for two years, reported on how much of the "dossier" had been corroborated. Without, of course, any specifics as to what, exactly had been "corroborated." A word, by the way, that got a real workout by MSNBC and CNN. Among others.

It turned out to be all smoke. A long and expensive special counsel investigation by Robert Mueller did not find any corroboration and Inspector General Horowitz drove the final nail in the coffin of the "dossier" when he concluded, in his report, he had been only able to confirm the accuracy of a limited number of circumstantial facts, most of which were in the public domain, such as the dates that Carter Page traveled to Russia, the timing of events, and the occupational positions of individuals referenced in the reports."

The justification for issuing the warrants may have been flawed—and even criminally so—but that didn't stop the FBI from conducting the surveillance. But the warrants had expiration deadlines and had to be reissued. And the head of the NSC was in a position to know about it when that happened.

And if that had been General Flynn ... well, he would have early on asked questions that would not just blow up the whole Crossfire Hurricane project, but expose the criminality of the whole FBI team of McCabe, Strozk, Page and the rest. People would have been fired and would have even gone to jail.

So Flynn had to be removed. And he was.

Instead, McMaster was in. Someone who conferred regularly with Andrew McCabe, and who brought Eric Ciaramella into the West Wing, where he would author a famous email to John Kelly, one cited in the Mueller report, that claimed there was circumstantial evidence "Putin directed Trump to fire Comey." Total nonsense, but key to the frenzied drive to launch a Special Counsel investigation. The media went crazy with it.

My colleagues, who did know and did care, made sure that others found out. These others were in a position to do something. They included people at the White House and on Capitol Hill. Notably, they included Congressman Devin Nunes who first made the Crossfire Hurricane operation public and was savaged by the media as a consequence.

But he eventually was vindicated by the Horowitz report, which demolished the whole, elaborate coverup of Crossfire Hurricane, leaving its supporters with no defense but their own vaunted self-esteem and their bottomless gall. Still, they must now wait to see what would come next; at this writing, a criminal investigation that is being conducted by US Attorney John Durham.

The shock waves from the explosion of Crossfire Hurricane are still expanding and will likely take down many more of the people who ran it and covered it up.

As for the people who exposed it …

They, like me, were booted out of the NSC on one pretext or another. Or, in some cases, just because.

I was fired for writing a memo in which I made the case – obvious for anyone with eyes to see—that the President was being subverted.

The memo was my idea.

What did I hope to accomplish by writing it?

Well, first I wanted to get the attention of people who might have some influence with the President when it came to personnel issues. As I have written earlier, this was where the Trump Administration was most disastrously sabotaging itself. People who should have been dismissed were kept on. And people who should have been brought in and were not, in favor of people who should never even been considered.

No question, this was the greatest mistake of the Trump administration.

Some of us saw this very early. From the first days, in fact. I remember telling some people who were celebrating in the days immediately following the election, "You need to cool it. You haven't won anything, yet. You are in the boats, headed for the Omaha Beach, and the real fight is just about to begin."

In the days between the election and the Inauguration, I wrote a memo to Ginni Thomas, in which I listed people who needed to be gotten rid of right away if the Trump administration was to have any chance of success.

Many of those people were still there when I went to the NSC, and I soon found many more like them.

It seemed to me that the Trump administration had no chance unless someone got the attention of people who could make the necessary changes in personnel.

So I went to work on that other memo, which I hoped might eventually be read by…well, I suppose I hoped that it might eventually make it to the President's office. But short of that, there was Bannon. Maybe Jared.

I worked at home. At night. Over maybe two or three weeks. And when it was ready, I printed it at work to share with a few colleagues. Which meant it was logged in to the system.

The reason for this unorthodox staffing approach, circumventing the chain of command, is that I had learned not to trust McMaster and the various layers of staff between myself and the Oval Office. How could I?

I passed it around to the right people and it did, in fact, make it to the desks of Bannon and Jared. And, eventually, allegedly, the President read it while he was on Air Force One. I'm told he reacted enthusiastically.

This was exactly what I had wanted. But, like they say, "be careful what you wish for."

Allegedly, the President called in McMaster and told him, essentially, to start addressing the issues I'd identified. And although I didn't specifically name him in the memo, I suspect McMaster knew the memo was really about him and his beloved holdovers.

And at this point, my story with the NSC winds down. Quickly. I got called down to the NSC's Office of Legal Counsel.

Did I write this memo?

Yes. Of course.

And from there, after some debate amongst the lawyers, it goes on to a predictable sort of end, in which Jim Carroll, a Bush guy who had served as Karl Rove's Deputy, and is currently the head of the Office of National Drug Control Policy, signed the letter authorizing my termination. I got fired from my job for...well, for doing my job. For serving the President. I kept my security clearance and I got an ugly green bag to hold my personal stuff.

It was over…but, of course, it wasn't.

The people who were my allies, my fellow insurgents, were also run out of the NSC. The Deep State appeared to have prevailed, once again.

We all know much of what followed. The Crossfire Hurricane story exploded and for months the news was NOT about how the FBI had been extensively and illegally surveilling Americans, including the President, after deceiving the FISA court in order to obtain the necessary warrants.

It was, instead, about Trump and the "Steele Dossier" and Robert Mueller and "collusion."

If you didn't know what you were looking at during that time, then it appeared that Trump would, like me and the other NSC insurgents, soon be out.

Clapper, Brennan, Comey, Hayden…they were the winners. And Trump would be lucky to finish one term, much less be re-elected to a second.

Then, we heard from Horowitz. And soon we will hear from Durham. The entire "collusion" narrative collapsed. McCabe, Strozk, and Page are out. Schiff was exposed as a liar. Nunes as the truth teller.

But it hasn't ended. Trump is still under fire and he will be for as long as he is in the White House. If he gets a second term, this thing will go on. As it will, no matter what happens to Trump.

The Deep State isn't going away quietly.

As Bannon said at the CPAC in 2017, "if you thought they were going to give you the country back without a fight, you are sadly mistaken."

THE MEMO CONTINUED Political warfare is warfare.

Political warfare operates as one of the activities of the "counter-state" and is primarily focused on the resourcing and mobilization of the counter state or the exhaustion and demobilization of the targeted political movement.

18

ONCE MORE INTO THE BREACH

I had never thought that I would use much of what I knew about irregular warfare in America. These were skills for "over there." At least that's what I had thought.

God and life are funny that way. An old friend from the Pentagon used to say to me, "You're always where you're supposed to be." I was where I was supposed to be at the NSC where, along with some of my colleagues, the unraveling of Crossfire Hurricane began. And where, just possibly, the recovery of the Trump administration became possible. Although it certainly didn't look that way at first.

My colleagues and I were out and that made news for a few days. I turned down some requests for interviews when it was plain, I was just being set up. That I would be made out to be some sort of extremist kook who saw preposterous conspiracy where it didn't exist and ignored the obvious threat of Russian "collusion," that everyone in the mainstream could recognize. The media party line in those days was "Mueller…collusion with Russia…impending impeachment."

Things were so crazy that the cable networks were making time, it seemed like almost every night, for a charlatan and con man named Michael Avenatti. He was a lawyer and he made a lot of noise about how he was going to put Trump in prison and then maybe even run for President, himself. The pretty faces on cable where cheering him on. Until, that is, he got busted for extortion.

Avenatti is now doing time in prison. Trump is still in the White House and, finally, fighting back.

But that was still a long way off, back in the days after my dismissal. The people who thought of themselves as "the resistance" were in the saddle and riding for impeachment. And I was, pretty quickly, old news.

But I wasn't going away and I hoped Trump wasn't either. That he would continue to be a fighter and that, in time, the story of Crossfire Hurricane – the coup attempt to bring him down – would lead the news and he would get the MAGA train back on the tracks.

As time went by, I did a little of what you could call "friendly media." In particular, an interview with Monica Crowley for *The Hill.* The crux of that one was when I told her that Trump's enemies, within his own administration:

"… aim … to kill the issues he was elected on. We're still in Afghanistan. We don't have the border wall or even funding for it. We still have ObamaCare … the DOJ and FBI are leaving the rule of law in tatters while the Republican establishment allows a nearly 18-month-long unprecedented, extra-legal [special counsel Robert] Mueller spectacle to continue unabated. Mueller's deep-state rear-guard action exists to cover the retreat of corrupt officials."

That was probably the most public thing I did for the first year, year and a half. I was keeping my head down but I was still in the fight.

Steve Coughlin and I formed a non-profit think tank called *Unconstrained Analytics,* which we describe on our website as:

" A 501(c)3 dedicated to analysis of evidence unconstrained by preconceptions and biases. This includes thorough analysis of an enemy's threat doctrine unconstrained by bias, preconceptions and influence operations coming from the same."

From the beginning, I have believed that it is important for people to realize that what we are engaged in is not politics in the ordinary sense of horse trading and deal making and the rest. This is warfare.

Information warfare, legal warfare, economic warfare and *ultimately* political warfare.

Our enemies understand this.

We are reluctant to do so and our enemies know this as well. Sometimes from a sort of good natured, American innocence or naiveté. We haven't ever been through a Russian Revolution, or its equivalent. We need to learn the rules and understand the shape of the battlefield. Urgently.

Do you think that COVID-19 pandemic response was an isolated event that just happened to come along? Don't be naïve!

Spygate failed. Russiagate failed. Ukrainegate failed. Impeachment failed.

Did you think after the failed impeachment the Deep State was going to throw up their hands and say, "you won"?

No, they seamlessly moved into forcing President Trump to close down the largest economy in the world and print trillions of dollars. The financial elite control nations through debt. The national debt stands at $25 trillion and counting. The chickens will come home to roost sooner than later.

And this was all for a virus that has an infection mortality rate that is similar to the flu.

The pandemic response was an unprecedented escalation of political warfare by the Deep State against President Trump and against the American people.

Don't be a fooled that the response was done out of an abundance of caution. Events of this magnitude don't just happen.

Prior to COVID-19, the CDC and WHO did not recommend lockdowns, even for the most severe of pandemics. What changed? I will let you answer this question.

In addition to the think tank, I have made my living doing private sector work of the sort that has kept me busy these last two decades. Technical and analytic stuff.

And, then…I have stayed in the fight where it seemed like I could be useful. I worked with Congressman Devin Nunes and his staff, putting together what the Horowitz report would reveal as the true story of Crossfire Hurricane. As opposed, that is, to the fiction and lies that Congressman Adam Schiff assembled and peddled, successfully, to an eagerly complicit media. The work of Nunes and his staff—and the people, like me and my old colleagues who helped and contributed—is of historical importance. And may, in fact, have prevented a coup and saved a presidency.

Devin Nunes is a true national hero.

As I write, we may be witnessing the turning of the tide. It appears that President Trump and those close to him have come to realize the mistakes they made, what Bannon called the administration's "original sin," when they staffed the administration with people whose loyalty was not to the President or the issues he had campaigned on but to themselves and their security within the Deep State.

I never went into my shell. I don't, in fact, have a shell. Wouldn't be comfortable in one. To the degree I went silent, I also went deep. And lately, with the release of the Horowitz report and what I suspect will soon be the Durham indictments of some very senior people, I have been going increasingly public.

First, on Twitter, where the fight never ends and there is always something new that needs to be said, in the pithiest possible way. If I have a unique angle on something in the news, I go to Twitter.

And, of course, I have been working on this book.

Then, there are what might be called "discussions," with people I am not at liberty to name. The point of these talks is to go back and correct some of the mistakes I have described in these pages and to continue the fight to *Make American Great Again*.

That is what I enlisted for in the first place. And why I recently re-upped and remain avid supporter of Donald Trump in the 2020 election.

So for now…the battle for America goes on.

And the best is yet to come.

THE MEMO CONTINUED Attacks on President Trump are not just about destroying him, but also about destroying the vision of America that lead to his election. Those individuals and groups seeking the destruction of President Trump actually seek to suffocate the vision of America that made him president. Hence, the end state is not just a delegitimized, destabilized, immobilized and possibly destroyed presidency; but also a demoralized movement composed of a large enough bloc to elect a president that subsequently becomes self-aware of its own disenfranchisement.

APPENDIX

POTUS & POLITICAL WARFARE
May 2017

I. BACKGROUND. The Trump administration is suffering under withering information campaigns designed to first undermine, then delegitimize and ultimately remove the President. This is not politics as usual but rather political warfare at an unprecedented level that is openly engaged in the direct targeting of a seated president through manipulation of the news cycle.

II. INTRODUCTION. Responding to relentless personal assaults on his character, candidate Trump identified the players and the strategy:

- "The establishment and their media enablers will control over this nation through means that are very well known. Anyone who challenges their control is deemed a sexist, a racist, a xenophobe, and morally deformed." – President Trump, Oct 2016

While opposition to President Trump manifests itself through political warfare memes centered on cultural Marxist narratives, this hardly means that opposition is limited to Marxists as conventionally understood. Through the campaign, candidate Trump tapped into a deep vein of concern among many citizens that America is at risk and is slipping away.

Political Warfare. As used here, "political warfare" does not concern activities associated with the American political process but rather **exclusively** refers to political warfare as understood by the Maoist Insurgency model. Political warfare is one of the five components of a Maoist insurgency. Maoist methodologies employ synchronized violent and non-violent actions that focus on mobilization of individuals and groups to action. This approach envisions the direct use of non-violent operational arts and tactics as elements of combat power.

Political warfare is warfare. Strategic information campaigns designed to delegitimize through disinformation arise out of non-violent lines of effort in political warfare regimes. They principally operate through narratives. Because the hard left is aligned with Islamist organizations at local, national and international levels, recognition should be given to the fact that they seamlessly interoperate through coordinated synchronized interactive narratives.

Cultural Marxism. While the attacks on President Trump arise out of political warfare considerations based on non-violent lines of effort, they operate in a battle-space prepared, informed and conditioned by cultural Marxist drivers. In practical terms, the political warfare assault on President Trump cannot be separated from the cultural Marxist narratives that drive them. From an operational preparation of the environment perspective, President Trump is operating in a battle-space that reflects the left's vision.

As cultural Marxist narratives intensify, they are to be further operationalized in the form of hate speech narratives. Hate speech narratives are non-random, coordinated, and fully interoperable escalations of cultural Marxist memes. Key international players driving this phenomenon include the European Union, the UN, and the OSCE, the OIC and the International Muslim Brotherhood. Hate speech memes are structured, coordinated, and implemented through these same international forums. They involve close coordination with media and social media and include the Countering Violent Extremism (CVE) narratives.

Battlespace. These attack narratives are pervasive, full spectrum and institutionalized at all levels. They operate in social media, television, the 24-hour news cycle in all media, and are entrenched at the upper levels of the bureaucracies and within the foreign policy establishment. They inform the entertainment industry from late night monologues, to situation comedies, to television series memes, to movie themes. The effort required to direct this capacity at President Trump is little more than a programming decision to do so. The cultural Marxist narrative is fully deployed, pervasive, full spectrum and ongoing. Regarding the president, attacks have become a relentless 24/7 effort.

III. ENEMY CAMPAIGN PLAN.

A.) LINES OF EFFORT: Political Warfare has been described as "propaganda in battledress." The effort directed at President Trump is executed along one overt, as well as four covert, lines of effort:

- The overt line of effort is **PUBLICITY.** Publicity is the straightforward projection of a case that builds a picture in the audience's mind designed to garner support. It is facts without context and information the adversary wants the audience to possess that creates an impression and sets conditions. It seeks to establish good will and receptiveness to additional inputs.

- There are four covert lines of effort: **PROPOGANDA, AGITATION, PSYCHOLOGICAL OPERATIONS and INFILTRATION/SUBVERSION.**

  □ **Propaganda** is the deliberate direction, even manipulation, of information to secure a definite outcome. It is an attempt to direct the thinking of the recipient, without his conscious collaboration, into predetermined channels that are established in the Publicity line of effort. It is the unwitting conditioning of the recipient by devious methods with an ulterior motive that seeks to move them incrementally over time into greater belief and acceptance of message transmitted in the Publicity line of effort.

▫ **Agitation** is the purposeful exploitation of grievances (real or perceived, true or false) thru events or incidents that reinforce narratives at all levels. It is done in order to strengthen the impact of the propaganda and to create individual, group and societal level action in support of the perpetrators intended outcomes.

▫ **Psychological Operations** is the direct targeting of individuals and individual leaders based on remotely identified and/or assumed psychological vulnerabilities. The attackers find vulnerable points in the targeted individual and create narratives that seek to entice the targeted individual into actions inimical to his or her own interests. Some outcomes of these types of attacks, which are normally conducted through the media, include; trust erosion, ego fracture, paranoia, and isolation.

▫ **Infiltration and subversion** operate internal to the targeted organization in order to inform, target, coordinate, and amplify the effects of the publicity and propaganda. Both operate to gather intelligence, obstruct legitimate courses of action, provide inside information, and leak sensitive information that undermines the leadership and suppresses the morale of friendly elements.

　　* **Infiltration** of political and social groups within a target state is done for the purpose of extending counter-state influence and control. The endgame is concealed and may involve illicit activities.

　　* **Subversion** undermines or detaches the loyalties of significant political and social groups within the target

state and transfers political and/or ideological loyalties to the counter-state. As the counter-state forms, a counter-elite of influential individual and key leaders within the target state will later facilitate the legitimacy and permanency of the new regime.

B.) NARRATIVES. Political warfare employs publicity, propaganda, and psychological operations. It recognizes no intrinsic virtue in the news but rather envisions it as a mechanism to exploit. From a political warfare perspective, control of the news cycle is the most potent means of attracting and building up a favorable audience as well as delegitimizing the opposition and its related movements. As it relates to the news cycle, publicity and propaganda can be merged to form a "pseudo-publicity" that is presented as news in furtherance of sustaining pseudo-realities maintained by cultural Marxist memes. Pseudo-publicity treatment of President Trump dominates the news cycle. The current campaign against President Trump operates in the following manner:

The Meta Narrative. Meta narratives seeks to delegitimize President Trump, his administration, and the vision of America he projected as a candidate. With cultural Marxist memes serving as the backdrop, President Trump is to be relentlessly characterized as unfit through the use of supporting narratives acting to move unwitting populations to belief in the meta narrative. Hence:

- "President Trump is illegitimate"

- "President Trump is corrupt"

- "President Trump is dishonest"

Note that the twitter accounts and mainstream media personalities pushing this narrative have seen their audience numbers rise greatly in the past 6 months. This is a direct result of the supporting and backdrop narratives channeling individuals to this meta-narrative.

Supporting Narratives. Meta-narratives are supported by an ongoing series of supporting-narratives that can be swapped out as circumstances warrant. It is important to recognize that these stories do not have to be true, valid or accurate to serve their purpose. Over time, deserved or not, the cumulative effect of these supporting narratives will result in a Trump fatigue. From a political warfare perspective, President Trump's inability to meet this challenge will cast him as a weak failed leader. The current list of supporting narratives include:

- "Russia hacked the election" - illegitimate

- "Obstruction of Justice"- corrupt

- "Hiding Collusion" - dishonest

- "Putin Puppet" - treasonous

Backdrop Narratives. The backdrop to the meta and supporting narratives are cultural Marxist memes designed to sustain a general sense of loathing of President Trump and the America that elected him. Hence:

"[*meta*] President Trump is illegitimate, [*supporting*] he was elected because of Russian hacking, [*backdrop*] and besides, he a racist, sexist xenophobe."

Adversaries utilize these interlocking narratives as a defensive political and information warfare screen that silences critics and smears supporters of President Trump. When people in the media question the behavior, actions and decisions of the Trump Administration's opponents, they are immediately said to be "working for the Russians" or "supporting Russian propaganda." Individual Americans who support the President are deemed "deplorable" and "racist."

C.) END STATE. Attacks on President Trump are not just about destroying him, but also about *destroying the vision of America that lead to his election*. Those individuals and groups seeking the destruction of President Trump actually seek to suffocate the vision of America that made him president. Hence, the end state is not just a delegitimized, destabilized, immobilized and possibly destroyed presidency; but also *a demoralized movement composed of a large enough bloc to elect a president that subsequently becomes self-aware of its own disenfranchisement.*